WINE

B·A·S·I·C·S

A Quick and Easy Guide

DEWEY MARKHAM, JR.

Foreword by Robert Mondavi

John Wiley & Sons, Inc.

New York / Chichester / Brisbane / Toronto / Singapore

Publisher: *Tom Woll*
Editor: *Claire Thompson*
Managing Editor: *Jacqueline A. Martin*
Editorial Production: *David denBoer, Nighthawk Design*

This text is printed on acid-free paper.

Library of Congress Cataloging-in-Publication Data

Markham, Dewey
    Wine basics: a quick and easy guide/by
Dewey Markham, Jr.
        p.   cm.
    Includes bibliographical references and index.
    ISBN 0-471-58258-1 (pbk. : alk. paper)
    1. Wine and wine making.   I. Title.
TP248.M343   1993
641.2'2—dc20   92-27315

Printed in the United States of America
20 19 18 17 16 15 14 13

Contents

Foreword

Dewey Markham's *Wine Basics* is approachable and satisfying—just like a fine wine. He takes a commonsense path to enjoying wine by advising readers to treat wine like any other food: experiment a little, decide for yourself which wines and wine styles you like best, and then learn more about winegrowing to increase your appreciation and enjoyment. Unfortunately, over the years, we wine producers have created a mystique about wine that often leads to an elitist or snob image around our product. Nothing could be further from the truth! Wine is a natural agricultural product that has been part of our civilized world for more than 7,000 years; it is a mealtime beverage of moderation for enjoyment at the family table, as well as more elaborate celebrations.

At our winery in the Napa Valley, it's great fun watching first-time visitors taste wine seriously for the first time, and seeing their enjoyment and pleasure. Tasting without any preconceptions about what they should like and why, they are much more open to trying different varietals and deciding their preference.

As the quality of our American wines has evolved over the past 25 years, placing our wines in the company of the world's wines, there has been renewed interest in wine worldwide. While we've made great progress in recent years, I say the best is yet to come! We will accomplish more in the next five years than we have in the past 15 years as we learn more and more about growing wines naturally in our vineyards. Today our California wines are much more elegant, much more balanced, and much more expressive of our great climate and soil than those "Powerhouse" wines we produced in the 1970s. Today our wines are much more gentle, harmonious and flavorful, wines that are more accessible while young, yet have great aging potential. These are wines that truly enhance, not overpower, the foods they are paired with.

Fueling this increased interest in wine are numerous medical studies recently reported by the media that confirm that for most people wine enjoyed in moderation is not only good, but good for you.

Dewey Markham's book re-enforces the simple pleasures a bottle of wine brings at the table with good food, good friends and family. He takes the mystery, which often alienates new wine drinkers, out of wine, while retaining the romance that makes wine unique.

To your health!

Robert Mondavi

Preface

Wine is one of the most elegant of human creations. It is unparalleled in enhancing the enjoyment of a fine meal, imparting a spirit of refinement to any occasion, and offering a complexity of character that is unlike that available from any other beverage.

Wine is a good, basic, everyday drink. A glass with lunch or dinner adds a nice touch, and you don't have to save it for any special occasion. It provides an enjoyable change of pace from the beverages that we usually have with food.

Wine is a great party drink. It tastes good, you can get it in jugs or "on tap" in a bag-in-a-box, and it doesn't have to cost you an arm and a leg to pour a decent glass for a party, a picnic, or any kind of get-together.

These are three generally held attitudes regarding wine that are all equally valid. And then there's a fourth, which sounds something like this:

Wine is for snobs. It's too complicated to enjoy, it tastes funny, you have to know a bunch of rules like what type to drink with what food, and if you don't know the rules you look like a jerk. Besides, it costs too much to get something decent, and I don't eat fancy or have special occasions to drink it with. Gimme another soda, Harry.

As valid as the first three attitudes are, this last one is so far from being reasonable that it's hard to know where to begin to try and set things straight. But setting things straight is the aim of this book, and even if you find yourself more closely in line with one of the first three attitudes, you'll still find that what's presented here can help you gain a better understanding of just what wine appreciation is about and how it can help you better enjoy your wine of choice, whatever it may be.

This book is written with the aim of helping you become a better wine drinker, to enjoy wine regardless of what you drink and when you drink it, and to give you the skill, knowledge, ability, or whatever else you think you need in order to avoid, as the French put it, "drinking dumb"—that's to say, not getting your money's worth from a bottle of wine.

The information and principles in this book will apply to practically any wine you may encounter, no matter where it is made. You don't have to know French, Italian, German, or any other language to understand anything in the pages that follow, just as you don't have to understand any particular language to enjoy wine. And even if you've never pulled a cork or unscrewed the cap from a bottle of wine, everything here will be explained in such a way that you should be left with fewer questions, not more.

Above all, I hope that reading this book will allow you to feel at ease with wine, whenever you decide to open a bottle. Remember, just because wine is an integral part of many religious ceremonies (there are some wines whose taste can be like having a religious experience, but that's not the same thing), this doesn't mean that you always have to drink it on bended knees.

Acknowledgments

As an American I grew up and lived most of my adult life with little awareness and much suspicion of wine. Although I was fairly comfortable about food, having received the finest available education at The Culinary Institute of America, my appreciation of wine lagged far behind.

Then I went to Paris, where I became director of students at Ecole de Cuisine La Varenne, and during my three years in France I was surrounded by a culture in which wine was more than just an accompaniment to lunch and dinner; it was a natural and enriching part of daily life. Under such circumstances it was impossible to remain immune to its influence, and I began to feel more at ease as I saw that it did not require any esoteric knowledge or a refined attitude to enjoy a glass or two with dinner. It is this uncomplicated approach to wine held by millions of people around the world that I have tried to present in this book.

Although my appreciation of wine was a personal development it was by no means a solitary endeavor; and so this book, which is the product of that development, owes its existence to a number of people.

Foremost among them is Chef Patrick Cirotte and his charming wife Mireille, proprietors of the Parisian restaurants *Le Grenadin* and *Berry's*. Their kindness and generosity in Paris and their extraordinary hospitality in their native Sancerre were the catalysts behind my deeper interest in wine. While a guest of the Cirottes one memorable weekend in the Loire, I made the acquaintance of two fine winemakers, Didier Dagueneau of Pouilly-sur-Loire and Vincent Pinard of Bué, who explained what they did with a clarity and passion that literally changed my life. To all of these people I shall be forever grateful. No less influential has been Christian Martray, *Meilleur Jeune Sommelier de Bourgogne,* former *sommelier* at Le Grenadin, and now a cherished friend who teaches me more about wine each time we open a bottle together.

Here in America, my appreciation goes out to Lou Fiore of West Park Wine Cellars in the Hudson Valley of New York, for always opening wide the winery doors for me throughout the years. I also wish to thank Bill Cadelik, as well as Richard Nagel and Nikos Antonakeas of Morrell & Company for one very enlightening Christmas season; and particularly Michael Aaron and Michael Yurch of Sherry-Lehmann Wines and Spirits, who gave me the opportunity to continue my vinological education as a wine advisor in what is surely the Harvard of American wine shops for employees and customers alike.

Thanks are also due to Marie-Anne Dufeu for her generous help at a crucial stage of this book's development, and to Philip Spitzer, my agent, for his belief in the success of this project. I am very grateful to Michael Bartlett of *Restaurants & Institutions* magazine for shepherding the manuscript to John Wiley & Sons, and particularly to Claire Thompson, my editor, whose suggestions and guidance have made this a much better book.

But most of all I thank my sister, whose creation of "The Cathy J. Markham Fund for the Support of Wine Writers Who Happen to Be Her Brother" made the writing of this book possible. More than anyone else, this book owes its existence to her.

1

Introduction

There's something about wine that makes perfectly intelligent, capable people doubt their capacity for sound judgment. More often than not, it isn't acknowledged, and it may not even be given a lot of thought. But all the same, for many people the idea of choosing a wine in a store or restaurant is akin to taking the SAT.

Let's face it. This is not a matter of life or death, and 100 years from now no one is ever going to know what wine you choose. Still, there seems to be enough doubt involved in the decision to send the sales of bottled water soaring as the "smart" alternative to soda pop.

Occasionally, a person will make a tentative effort to see what all the fuss is about, and will look in a book that explains what makes wine so special. Sooner or later there's always a paragraph that reads something like this: "Wine is one of the most complex foods known to humankind. Each possesses a unique character, the result of a myriad of chemical compounds believed to number in the thousands, of which scientists have succeeded in identifying only around 100, and each compound contributes something indefinable and often unforgettable to a wine's complexity of taste and aroma." Words like this tend to make one feel that it's necessary to pass an entrance exam just to step foot in a wine shop.

And then, to back this up, there is the popular image of The Wine Expert who sniffs at a glass and comes out with: "A most subtle array of sensory impressions, with a thick carpet of raspberries and rose petals in the forefront, which is nicely complemented by a deeper imprint of cedar and Russian leather, all of which clearly indicate that the wine is from a good year, but nearing its peak of drinkability." And so on. And the guy hasn't even *tasted* the stuff yet.

Well to begin with, wine *is* made up of a lot of complex components. But so is an automobile, yet you don't feel the need to avoid cars and buses just because you don't know what all those gears and pistons are doing down there beneath the hood.

And then all that rigmarole about raspberry rugs and the rest can be boiled down to just two simple sentences: "I like this wine" or "I don't like this wine." There's nothing particularly complicated about that, now, is there? Chances are good that you've already used these phrases about other things. Just change the last word and see how familiar it sounds: "I like this music"; "I don't like this painting"; "I like this comedian"; "I don't like this color."

"Ah, but it's not so simple," you may say. "With wine we're talking about *taste*, and that's a lot more subtle than the question of whether a joke is funny or if blue is as nice as red. Remember, 'wine is one of the most complex foods known to humankind.'"

All right, all right. Everything we eat or drink is pretty complex, and if it's not to begin with, then we make it so before we put it in our mouths—that's what cooking and bartending are all about. A couple of examples will show that we are already quite capable of making subtle distinctions of quality based on our sense of taste.

Remember "The Pepsi Challenge"? Those ads in which people just like you and me preferred one cola over the other? And how about all the fuss over "New Coke" versus "Classic Coke"? In both cases, millions of Americans were clearly able to distinguish and express a distinct personal preference for one or another of two very similar products. Substitute wines for colas and you've got your basic, every-day wine expert. That's really all there is to it.

Just about anybody is perfectly capable of thinking about wines as they do about soft drinks—or potato chips, or ketchups, or beers, or any other foodstuff. But there's a bit of a Catch-22 behind the difficulty people have when it comes to wine: you can't really think intelligently about something that you don't bother with because you don't believe you can have any intelligent thoughts about it. Got that? You'll finally have to come to grips with it: the only way you're ever going to know enough to be able to say, "I'll have this wine, because I like it," is simply by starting to drink wine.

Fortunately, few things in life are as pleasant, so let's begin.

CHEERS! _____

The goal of this book is to increase your understanding and enjoyment of this subject by presenting basic information applicable to virtually any wine you are likely to encounter, regardless of its origin or the type of grape from which it was made. By focusing on winemaking principles instead of regions of production and on fundamentals of taste instead of grape varieties, the entire world of wine should become less mysterious and more pleasurable.

But to understand the universal it often helps to look at the specific, so throughout this book you'll find special "Cheers!" sections containing recommendations of particular types of wine that will best illustrate the topic under discussion in the accompanying text. It's by actual tasting that you'll come to understand such points as what is meant by a sweet or a dry wine, or how different ways of treating grapes during wine-making will affect the finished product. Written explanations may make sense on their own, but a sip of wine can make their significance unforgettable.

In these sections we recommend that you taste not just one, but two or more wines together. While any one of the wines will adequately illustrate the given point in question, comparing it with others of contrasting qualities will more than double your understanding. After all, how would we know what bitter was like if all we ever tasted was sweet?

And since *particular wines* are often difficult to find due to regional distribution patterns and individual retailer preferences, *representative types* of wine are recommended. The wines whose labels appear in these sections are offered only as suggestions. They possess characteristics representative of their type, and were chosen because of their wide availability and good value. If you can find these wines, fine; if not, simply substitute others of the same type. Your understanding of the point in question should be the same.

2

Why Drink Wine?

There are any number of answers to this question, and in this chapter we'll look at some of them. Some people need no reason to drink wine, while others have several.

Utilitarian: "It keeps me from choking on my food."

Romantic: "The person I'm dining with will think I'm intelligent and sophisticated, so I'll probably score."

Stupid: "If I drink enough, I can get drunk."

Self-Improving: "I'll be a better, more cultured person for drinking wine instead of soda pop."

Impressionable: "They always drink wine in the fancy scenes in the movies."

Rich: "Because I can afford it."

Economical: "It was only $1.99."
Sociable: "The guy came up to me with all these glasses on a tray, so I took one."
Fraternal: "He's buying."

As you can see, there are numerous reasons people might cite for drinking wine. Now, any of these may be reason enough for uncorking a bottle, but none is as valid, none makes as much sense, and none will orient you better toward developing a true appreciation for wine as this: "It tastes good."

This, when all is said and done, is what wine drinking is about. There is no law that says anyone must drink wine with a meal (although there have been laws to prevent it). From a purely functional point of view, water will wash food down your throat and prevent choking just as effectively. But although water may be cheaper, wine tastes better. Wine has *flavor*, and not only can that flavor be attractive on its own, but it can also marry with and enhance the flavor of the food with which it is served. Look at it this way: if you're going from New York to Philadelphia, the bus will get you there; but making the trip in a Porsche is so much more pleasant.

We'll get to the combination of wine and food in Chapter 17. To keep things simple for now, we'll focus only on the taste of wine.

Wine has flavor, and that flavor should be good. But what constitutes good? This is a matter of personal taste, and regardless of what rating scores, comments, or judgments you may read or hear about a wine, remember that they are only opinions. You are under no obligation to take them as being more valid than your own. (In fact, when it comes to these expert opinions, the weight of obligation is really on the part of the experts to convince you of the validity of their views and their claim to the title "expert"; no obligation is on you to conform your tastes to theirs.)

When you buy a bottle of wine at a store or restaurant, you are not paying for the attractive label, the fact that it comes from a "name" area or winemaker, or any of the other trappings that are peripheral, but all too often central, to your choice. No, what you are paying for, very simply, is the wine's taste.

Given that what's important is taste, the question of value becomes a little better focused: the wine that is going to be good value for your money is the one that gives you the most taste per bottle. In other words, when you buy a bottle of wine, the taste should last as long as possible—from the time the first sip is taken to when the last drops are shaken out into the glass. This is not unlike the primary reason we buy so many other things: a car offers transportation, and its basic value is measured in how long it continues to provide it; we buy a light bulb for light, and the longer it can produce that, the better the bulb is.

Now, there are two ways that you can get more taste per dollar. One way is to buy larger bottles for the same price. The sizes of wine bottles, however, are regulated by law. Although you may occasionally see the odd one-liter container, the standard bottle holds 750 ml. Practically speaking then, this option is moot. The second way to get the most taste for your dollar is to pack more flavor into each sip, so that even after the wine has been swallowed its taste lingers;

when the taste finally dies away, another sip is then taken to stimulate the palate once again.

For example: let's suppose that in a bottle of wine there are 100 sips. Each time you take a sip and swallow it the taste lingers for three seconds; when the taste sensation of one sip has faded completely, you take another to return the taste to your mouth. Drinking the wine in this manner, the bottle will last you for 300 seconds (100 sips at three seconds per sip), or five minutes. Now let's take another bottle of wine, this time one whose taste lingers for six seconds per sip. This second wine will afford you 10 minutes of drinking pleasure—twice as much as the first.

This persistence of flavor is a primary indicator of quality in a wine. There is no need to go into a long description about a wine's aroma or layers of taste—all of that raspberry rug talk. Even if you've never tasted wine before, you can reach a basic conclusion regarding the quality of a wine: all that you need to do is to concentrate on the wine in your mouth and look at the secondhand of your watch. In our example we looked at the principle behind all this. Now let's see how it works in reality.

To begin, take a good-sized sip of wine. Now roll the liquid around, passing it over your gums, inside your cheeks, and across the roof of your mouth in order to bring it into complete contact with the taste receptors that will register the wine's flavor and intensity, and then swallow. You don't have to make faces or gargling noises, and it's not necessary to do this for longer than two or three seconds.

After swallowing, don't talk. Beware of those who start telling you what they think of a wine before it has even made it to their stomachs. You don't have to swallow again. Just concentrate on the flavor that remains from the traces of wine that you swirled around in your mouth, and start counting how many seconds that sensation lasts before it is washed away by newly produced saliva. The basic rule is: *The longer the taste lasts, the better the wine is.* And it's as simple as that.

We used the words "longer" and "better," which are comparative terms—longer and better than what? Than another wine of the same type.

Try this: get two bottles of the same type of wine—two Red Bordeaux, or two White Burgundies, or two Chiantis. Buy one with a price tag of about $3.99, and the other at a price of around $8 or $9. Pour each wine into its own glass. Starting with the less expensive wine, take a sip and count the length of time its taste lingers after swallowing. To avoid confusing your taste buds, let a little time pass before repeating this with the second wine. If there is any justice in the world and the secondhand of your watch is ticking consistently, you should find that the pricier wine lasts longer. All else being equal, it is therefore the better wine. (As a point of reference, simple table wines tend to have a duration of two to three seconds, and the taste of the finest—and most expensive—wines lasts up to ten seconds or longer. You may experience consistently longer or shorter times, however, due to differences in individual sensitivity, experience, etc.)

You see, the ability of a wine's taste to endure in the mouth doesn't happen by accident. It is the result of a conscious effort by the winemaker to produce a quality wine.

This effort takes money, and the extra cost to make a better wine will be reflected in the higher price tag on the bottle. Thus, in theory, the more you pay for a bottle of wine, the longer the taste should linger.

Now, this doesn't mean that you always have to spend a lot of money on a bottle of wine to assure yourself of getting something good to drink. There's nothing wrong with staying with wines in the $3.99 range; indeed, there are some excellent values. How to recognize them? Count how many seconds their aftertaste lasts. If you find a wine whose taste lingers much longer than the others of that type you've had, then you've made a discovery of a wine whose persistence of taste is equivalent to one that costs several dollars more.

Sometimes the opposite can be true: a wine will come from an area that is known for high quality, but the winemaker prefers to coast on the reputation of the area rather than spend the money necessary to make a really good wine. The price will be the same as the truly well-made wine, but the quality won't be there. How can you tell if you are getting the best value for your dollar? Count how many seconds the finish lasts and keep track of your count. The next time you have a wine of the same type, see which one comes up with the highest count. Then, if everything else about the wines was equally pleasing, stick with the one that gave you the longest count. (Of course, there are numerous factors that cause one wine to have a longer aftertaste than another; you mustn't think that every winemaker is a crook just waiting to be unmasked by a longer-lasting wine. There are any number of reasons why a wine may be longer- or shorter-lasting, many of which we will cover in the chapters that follow.)

When people refer to this characteristic of a wine, they will speak of a wine's *length of finish*. "This is a wine of some length," you may hear. Or, "It's very long on the finish." Conversely, you may hear, "It's a rather short wine," or "It has no length." So for now, if you feel the need to give an opinion about a wine you've just tasted and have always felt at a loss for something intelligent to say, you can always go with, "I like it; it has a nice, long finish." Or, "I don't care for it; it's rather short on the finish."

3

The Taste
of White Wine

So far we've spoken about the quality of a wine in terms of the length of time its taste lingers in the mouth after swallowing. You could use this as the sole criterion for judging a wine, forget about going any farther in this book, and still have a fairly reliable yardstick by which the quality of a wine may be judged. But there are other factors of a wine's taste that should be considered as well. After all, the taste of Drāno will linger in your mouth for a real long time, but I don't think that you'd consider it the perfect accompaniment with dinner for that reason. Length of taste is one aspect, but the character of that taste should also be considered. It's all well and good if the bulb in your bedside lamp lasts a long time, but if it is a 600-watt spotlight instead of a softer, more soothing light, length becomes somewhat less important.

We spoke earlier about all of the long and elaborate descriptions that are given when evaluating wines, the flowery language and the complicated appraisals. But when we are talking about white wines, it all comes down to considering just two basic aspects of flavor; for red wines, three.

In white wines, flavor is a balance of *sweetness* and *acidity*. Both of these are found in the grapes from which the wine is made. We all know that grapes are sweet; that's one of the reasons they are so popular as an eating fruit. The acidity is there too, although it is not one of the first things about grapes we may normally think of. It's the acidity that gives them that pleasant tartness that we find so refreshing. The way in which the grapes are handled during winemaking determines the balance of sweetness and acidity that will be evident in the finished wine. Ideally, that balance between the sugar and acid keeps the wine from being either too cloyingly sweet or too sharply tart.

The basic aspects of sweetness and acidity in white wines are not absolutes, but vary in intensity depending on the type of grapes used, the manner in which they were grown and vinified, and numerous other influences. Although the differences in taste are subtle and can range over an infinitely demarcated spectrum of intensity, we can distill it all down to a more manageable range of five levels of sweetness and five of acidity. For simplicity's sake these could be labeled numerically, like the Richter scale used for measuring earthquakes, but we must never forget that there is poetry in wine. So in place of numbers 1 through 5, more descriptive terms have been assigned to these sensations.

For sweetness, these five levels of intensity, from weakest to strongest, are identified as *hollow, little, watery, unctuous,* and *heavy.*

For acidity, the five levels of intensity (in ascending order) are *hollow, thin, meagre, tart,* and *aggressive.*

Now let's lay out these two scales (below) in order to get a visual idea of what we're talking about, arranging the sweetness scale vertically, the acidity scale horizontally.

The midpoint of each scale represents a balance between too much and too little sweetness or acidity in a wine. You will see that on our two scales we've drawn a line out from that point, dividing each in half. On the sweetness scale the area below the division contains the wines that to varying degrees are deficient in that quality; the area above the line is for those wines with a surfeit of sweetness.

Similarly, on the acidity scale the area to the left of the line will contain wines insufficiently acidic, while to the right will be found those wines that are overly so.

Finally, let's combine the two scales. The result gives us the scale on the next page. The point in the middle where

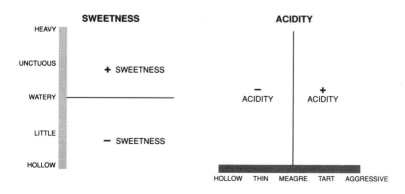

the two lines intersect represents a wine that is balanced in both sweetness and acidity; each of the four areas around it will be either weaker or stronger in these two basic characteristics.

As our combining of the two scales implies, neither sweetness nor acidity exists on its own in a white wine. There is an interplay between the two that produces a final sensation in the mouth that is clearly the product of both, yet is different enough to require its own descriptive term. The effect is to create something akin to a multiplication table of taste sensations on which you can easily find the appropriate name to put to the taste of any white wine. From the interplay of the five basic levels of sweetness and acidity, we get 25 terms that comprise the descriptive vocabulary for the taste of white wines.

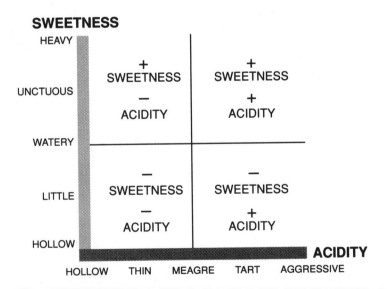

SWEETNESS

HEAVY	LIQUEUR-LIKE	HONEYED	FULL	NERVOUS
UNCTUOUS	SWEETISH	FAT	SUSTAINED	HARD
WATERY	LIMP	BALANCED	LIVELY	ACIDY
LITTLE	FLAT	DRY	FRESH	GREEN
HOLLOW	THIN	MEAGRE	TART	AGGRESSIVE

ACIDITY

Adapted from *Le Vin: Votre Talent de la Dégustation,* by Jean-Claude Buffin
(Doussard: Hobby-Vins, 1988).

And here you have it, the source of all that talk about lively Chardonnays and flat Chablis. Depending on the effect that a given white wine produces in the mouth, you can easily come up with an appropriate description of that sensation that will be readily understood by others. Each word is quite rich in its descriptive power, without going off the deep end into the florid metaphors that you occasionally find employed by wine writers. But let's take a closer look at the choice of words used and their positioning in the scale above.

These adjectives were chosen for their ability to convey a lot of meaning very economically. Therefore, it is rather simple to attach positive and negative connotations to each one. Clearly, you don't want to spend a lot of time and money on a wine that is flat, limp, or watery. It's all a matter of taste, but in general among the positive descriptions here would be balanced, dry, fat, honeyed, fresh, lively, sustained, and full.

Still, do not be misled by the term "balanced" and its central position in the scale. Balance is a quality that is ideal in the abstract, but wine is not an abstraction. There are wines that are meant to be rather sweet and others that are supposed to be quite acidic; it is in their nature to be so. Think of it like this: all beers are made from the same basic ingredients and are processed in the same basic way. Yet you wouldn't expect a light beer to taste like a regular brew, much less like the dry variety. You know when you pick up a beer labeled "dry" what to expect, and it is the same with wines. Some white wines like Chablis or Muscadet are vinified to be acidic in character, with a "fresh" or "lively" bite to them. Such a wine that approached "balanced" would be a disappointment, indicating that there was too much sweetness in the finished product.

In the same way, when we see the word "Sauternes" on a label (indicating a sweet dessert wine), we have every right to expect a wine whose taste is to be found toward the upper end of the sweetness scale: liqueur-like, honeyed, or fat.

The differences to be found in the taste of a particular type of wine is a result of the many variables that come into play in the production of a wine: the ripeness of the grapes (some grape growers harvest their grapes earlier than others); the location of the vineyard from which those grapes came (some parcels of land get more direct sunshine than others); and the individual skills and preferences of the winemaker (Pierre likes a little more sweetness, Jacques likes to emphasize the acidity). As long as the end result falls recognizably within the generally expected taste boundaries for that particular type of wine, there is nothing especially wrong with it. All of which leaves you with the pleasant task of tasting your way through the different styles of Chablis, Sauternes, or whatever to discover which ones suit your own personal preferences.

Of course, if you get a Sauternes that tastes fresh, lively, or dry, or a Chablis that is sweetish, fat, or honeyed, even though it may taste quite pleasant, clearly something is amiss. Then you share the predicament of the gentleman in the cartoon from *Punch*: "Look here, Steward, if this is coffee, I want tea; but if this is tea, then I wish for coffee."

Now in addition to what they offer in terms of taste, sweetness and acidity play secondary roles in defining the character of a wine.

During vinification the sugar content of a grape is transformed into several other substances, including that most interesting of by-products, alcohol. While not as sweet as the grape's original sugar, these substances remain to some degree recognizably sweet to the taste. But in addition to taste, they also contribute to the wine's body. This is what makes a wine more than just some flavorful concoction with the consistency of water.

Don't underestimate the importance of consistency in the enjoyment of a beverage. We've all had the experience of coming back to a cup of soda after the ice cubes in it have melted. To a certain extent the flavor has been weakened by the additional water from the melted ice, but what really makes the drink insipid is the dilution of the soda's usual syrupy consistency. Whether we are drinking soda, milk, beer, or wine, we expect the liquid to have a certain body. The more watery a liquid's consistency (unless, of course, that liquid is water), the more likely we are to consider it "weak," "thin," or "limp," and therefore less enjoyable.

In a white wine, acidity's secondary importance is more chemical than tactile. It is the acid in white wine that helps preserve it. The higher a wine's acid content, the longer its life will be.

Now why is this so important? Well, if wine had a shelf life no longer than a container of milk, you'd be continually running to the store for a bottle to have with lunch or dinner instead of simply going to your cellar or closet (or wherever you keep your wine) and pulling out a nice little something to go with your meal. You'll appreciate all that acid in your wine when you don't have to go out to the store some cold, rainy evening, believe me.

The other nice thing about prolonging the life of a wine is that with age its sweetness and acidity marry together to become more than their individual parts, like a good stew that gets better after it has sat in the fridge overnight. With wine, the longer you can manage to prolong its development, the better it will eventually taste. Climb to the top of a 500-foot hill and you can get a nice view for five miles; climb to the top of a 1000-foot mountain and you have a breath-taking view of 50. It takes longer to get there, but the payoff is worth it.

Okay, you say, if acidity in wine is so great, why don't they just pump in as much acid as possible and be done with it? Because, remember, we're talking about something you want to drink, not put into the battery of your car. It's okay to have a lot of acidity in a wine, as long as it is matched by an appropriate level of sweetness. That's the difference between a wine that's "tart" and one that's "sustained" or "full."

When it comes to buying wine, people will most often ask for reassurance on one particular point: "Is this a dry wine?" Popular opinion holds that sweet beverages are unsophisticated and the taste of people who drink them is similarly suspect, regardless of the fact that some of the most exquisite (not to mention expensive) wines in the world are by nature sweet.

But although dry wines are most often requested, some can be a bit too severe for many people. Fortunately, there is quite a range of tastes to choose from while still avoiding the

MISE AU   DOMAINE

CHABLIS

APPELLATION   CHABLIS   CONTROLÉE

12,5% Alc. Vol.   WHITE TABLE WINE   750 ml

DOMAINE DE LA MALADIÈRE
A CHABLIS · FRANCE   PROPRIÉTAIRE-RÉCOLTANT
PRODUCE OF FRANCE

SEAGRAM
IMPORTED BY (CHATEAU & ESTATE) NEW-YORK N.Y.
WINES CO.

Chablis, Domaine de la Maladière

dreaded label of "sweet." The suggestions below are just a few of the types that cover the basic spectrum of dry white wine styles. A comparison of these three types should help you determine the degree of dryness you prefer.

For an example of a very dry wine, try a Chablis or a Muscadet from France.

Typical of the medium-dry range of tastes are many wines made from the chardonnay grape.

The upper end of dryness, but still respectably shy of sweet, is represented by the taste of the very popular White Zinfandel wines.

For examples of wines at the sweet end of the taste spectrum, see the section dealing with dessert wines on page 70.

Muscadet de Sèvre et Maine, Clos les Hautes Bretonnières

Chardonnay, West Park

Chardonnay, Quail Run

SUTTER HOME

1991 CALIFORNIA
WHITE ZINFANDEL

VINTED AND BOTTLED BY SUTTER HOME WINERY
NAPA, CALIFORNIA 94589 BW 5525
ALCOHOL 9% BY VOLUME. CONTAINS SULFITES

White Zinfandel, Sutter Home

4

The Taste
of Red Wine

As we've seen, the taste of white wines is the product of an interplay between two aspects of its flavor, sweetness and acidity. Both of these are present in red wines too, but what distinguishes the taste of the latter is the presence of a third component: *tannin*.

What is tannin? This substance is found in the woody parts of the grapevine, as well as in the grape's skin and pips. Most tannin makes its way into red wine during the pressing of the grapes, when the juice is allowed to remain in prolonged contact with the skin and the stalks that held the bunches of grapes together. (In white wines this contact is kept to a minimum, so virtually no tannin at all is extracted by the juice.)

As in white wines, sweetness and acidity play much the same roles in the taste of reds, but what about tannin? Here it's not so much a question of taste, but rather a physical sensation in which your mouth dries out and puckers up, and a certain raspiness may be felt as the wine passes along to the back of your throat. Sounds really pleasant, right? Well, before you decide to confine your drinking to white wines, understand that depending on the way the tannin balances with the sweetness and acidity, its contribution can be not only very attractive, but may well be the element that makes a wine the object of adulation.

The taste of red wines can be mapped out in much the same way as for the taste of whites, using the scale on p. 16 as a starting point and overlaying the effect of tannin onto it.

Accordingly, we'll start with the two basic aspects of sweetness and acidity, but turning it on its side while keeping their relationship unchanged yields the scale below. Now we add the aspect of tannin, which contributes a new dimension and gives the taste of red wines a character all its own to get the scale on the next page.

ACIDITY   **SWEETNESS**

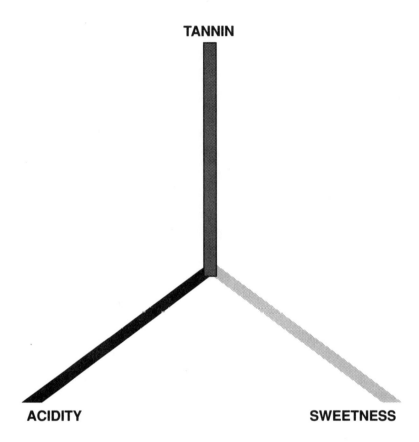

To underscore the difference between the tastes of red and white wines, we've used a triangle for the shape of the following scale, as opposed to the square shape that we used for the scale on p. 16.

Here equilibrium is found in the center, where the lines of sweetness, acidity, and tannin meet. A wine whose taste places it here has its three aspects in absolute balance. Of course, such a state in wine is the exception and not the rule; invariably, one or two of the three tastes will be more or less

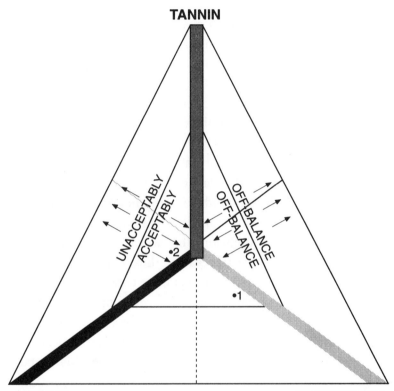

TANNIN

ACIDITY

SWEETNESS

pronounced, and this will move the wine's position away from the center to a certain degree.

The farther from the central point of balance we go along any of the three lines, the stronger that aspect of the wine's taste is. Conversely, if we follow any line toward the center and past the point of equilibrium, the weaker that aspect of the wine's taste is.

For example, if the acidity and sweetness in a wine's taste are both quite pronounced but the tannin is rather weak, the position of such a wine might be found around point 1. Similarly, if the tannin and sweetness are balanced but the acidity is predominant, the wine might be positioned around point 2 (see p. 29).

The important thing to remember is this: the stronger or weaker that one or two of the taste aspects of red wine are, the farther away from the central equilibrium point it will be found, and the more off-balance it is said to be. Within certain limits, the "off-balance" character of a wine is not particularly unpleasant; indeed, it might even give a certain interest to a wine. We can draw a boundary around the central point of equilibrium that will serve to delimit the acceptably off-balance wines from those that are too strong or weak in one or another aspect to be considered pleasing.

What we now have is merely a drawing; to make it a figure that we can use to help zero in on a description of a red wine's taste, we must add descriptive terms useful in defining the character of that taste. Again, there exist certain generally accepted adjectives that describe the various tastes of red wines, and we can simply plug these in to give us the next scale.

Here, then, is the graphic representation of the taste of red wines that we can use to assign a descriptive term to the sensation that a given red wine produces in the mouth. But what makes this scale so interesting is that it can be used not only to help define the taste of a given wine, but also to track its development.

You see, in addition to its primary effect on the taste of a red wine, tannin is also a determining factor in its ageability—not just how long a wine will take to reach its full

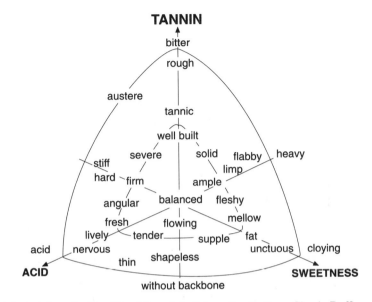

Adapted from *Le Vin: Votre Talent de la Dégustation*, by Jean-Claude Buffin (Doussard: Hobby-Vins, 1988).

potential, but how good it will be once it gets there and how long it will stay that way.

We spoke about why a long and happy life is desirable in a wine when we looked at acidity in white wines, and the same reasons hold true here: the longer it takes for a wine to pull its taste components into harmony, the finer the eventual taste will be. While acidity imparts (in both whites and reds) a certain longevity, it is tannin that really gives wine the ability to go the distance. This is readily seen when we compare the average life span of white wine with red. As an example, let's look at Château Margaux, one of the finest of French wine producers; although its renown is based on its red wine, the château makes a white wine too. The white will tend to reach its peak at around seven to eight years of age, while it is not at all unusual for the red wine to continue maturing for decades.

In a young red wine tannins can be harsh and off-putting, making it difficult to drink. But the same wine that is difficult to drink at three years of age can be smooth and inviting at ten. The effect of time on tannin is not unlike that of a river on the stones over which it flows—the roughness is worn smooth and sharp edges are rounded off. This is literally the difference in feeling that the mouth experiences. That abrasive, raspy character of which we spoke earlier becomes a full, silky sensation in the mouth that accounts for much of the greatness that is to be found in red wines. Tannins allow a red wine to age for a long time—but if we look at it another way, red wines *need* a long time to age *because* of the tannins in them. This is where the scale on p. 31 can become really useful.

We said earlier that this scale can be used not only to describe the taste of any red wine, but also to help us track its development. It works like this: as a red wine ages and its tannins mellow, the position at which the wine is to be found on the chart will shift vertically, descending in a straight line. The simplest illustration would be a wine whose acidity and sweetness are in balance, so as to position it directly on the TANNIN axis. If we first encounter the wine in its early youth, we may find it "bitter" or "rough." With time, however, the tannins will become more accessible, and the wine will be "tannic," then "well-built" in character. Further aging will produce a wine that is "balanced" or "flowing," which would be the optimum time for drinking. But if we allow the wine to continue aging it will descend into decrepitude as the tannins fade away altogether, becoming first "shapeless" and then finally "without backbone." Similarly, a wine that is on the acidic side might be "austere" in its youth and develop into a "firm," then "angular" and "fresh" wine during its peak period before becoming "thin" once it has gone over the hill.

Now, what good is this when you are sitting in a restaurant with a bottle of wine that you would describe as "severe"? Well, at least you have the satisfaction of knowing that had you had the good fortune to encounter that bottle a few years down the road it might have been a "tender" experience. But look at it this way: the tannins may have been a tad too underdeveloped for you then, but if everything else about the wine pleased you, you know that should you find and purchase a half-dozen bottles of it and lay them away, some enjoyable drinking awaits you in the future.

CHEERS!

There are a lot of wine drinkers who limit their choices to white wines; dealing with the astringency of tannin in red wines is something that they have just not been able to get used to. Fortunately, the amount of tannin in red wines varies, and finding one that is acceptably tender or supple should present little problem.

Beaujolais Nouveau, Georges Duboeuf

The prime candidate for a wine with easily accessible tannins is Beaujolais Nouveau. Available every year around the middle of November, this is an easy-drinking wine with the added attraction of being very reasonable in price. Depending on the demand, this wine should be readily available in wine shops throughout the winter months; the relay is then taken up by regular Beaujolais wine, which is available throughout the year beginning in the spring.

Beaujolais, Georges Duboeuf

Of course, there are certain charms to be found in a wine with a fuller complement of tannins, and these are nicely expressed in a wine such as a Chianti or (a little more expensively) a Barolo, both from Italy. Compared to the Beaujolais, these wines are more mouth-filling, and leave quite a substantial impression on the palate.

Chianti Classico, Rocca di Montegrossi

(In this example the less tannic wines happen to be French and the more tannic suggestions come from Italy, but it should not be surmised that this defines the character of every red wine produced in these two countries. Virtually every wine-producing nation makes numerous red wines of varying tannic character. By all means, experiment among the variety of wines that the world has to offer to discover the styles from each country that suit your taste.)

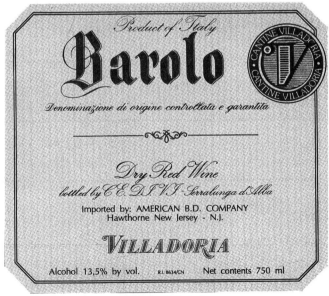

Barolo, Villadoria

5

The Smell of Wine

Okay, so now we have a basic handle on the taste of wines but you may be wondering about all that talk of raspberries, vanilla, and the variety of other descriptions that are so often used.

While all these things really can be found in a glass of wine, there are two main reasons we pass them by: (1) we don't know where to look, and (2) we have forgotten how to recognize them.

We don't know where to look. Just as when we listen to music we concentrate on what goes on in our ears, when we drink wine it's only natural to focus on what is happening in our mouths. Unfortunately, that's not necessarily the best place to find everything that a wine has to offer. Although various flavors in wine such as fruit and spices are picked up in the mouth, it is really through the sense of smell, not taste, that they are first and most strongly experienced. In short, our sense of smell plays a major role in our ability to taste.

Think back to the last time you had a head cold and your nose was stopped up. Chances are you didn't have much of an appetite and nothing seemed to taste right. The problem was not with your taste buds but with your sense of smell. The aromas of the food were unable to get through to the part of your nose that registers smells, and this had a direct effect on your sense of taste; without the added dimension of smell, everything was reduced to an unappetizing blandness. It's like having the TV on with the sound turned down. We speak of "watching" television, suggesting that it is just our sense of sight that is involved. But regardless of how sharp the picture or how large the screen, if you can't hear the TV set a lot of what is important gets lost and your pleasure in what you see is greatly reduced. It's the same thing with "tasting" wine.

We have forgotten how to recognize smells. To varying degrees, most of us have acquired the habit of closing off our sense of smell. It's a matter of self-defense, really. We are surrounded with smells continually; if we gave due attention to every one that came our way in the course of a day we would find ourselves overwhelmed by the amount of sensory information we'd have to process. So we get into the habit of not concentrating, and it is usually when someone specifically brings it to our attention ("Do you smell something burning?") that we focus on our sense of smell at all.

Consequently, we end up forgetting what things smell

like, and when we come across a smell that is detached from its traditional source, we may find that it is almost impossible to identify. To a lot of people the smell of an apple may be familiar but frustratingly unrecognizable until they see the apple and can anchor the smell to a visual reference.

This is what happens when we are presented with a glass of wine. When we raise it to the nose we know that there is a smell, but what is it? The only visual cue we have is a red or white liquid, which is not at all suggestive of what we are trying to identify. Unfortunately, we can't just say, "Oh, it smells like wine" and be done with it. There is something there that we have smelled before and until we can identify it it's like an itch that can't be scratched.

Now, there are people who have trained themselves to recognize the wide range of aromas to be found in wine, but for the most part these are professionals in the trade (wine-makers, buyers, wine waiters, etc.) who have refined their sense of smell to so high a degree because it is necessary for their work. They will search a wine's aroma for indications of defects in how it was made and whether it has the potential for greatness or mediocrity as it ages, two factors that can be important in fixing the price of large quantities of wine in the marketplace. Unfortunately, such an extreme level of sensitivity is all too often thought of as being integral to an appreciation of wine, which is not at all true; it would be like having to learn to pilot a Formula 1 racing car when all we want to do is drive down to the store for groceries. While such automotive skills are not absolutely necessary, we can still aspire to become better drivers.

When it comes to wine, we don't have to be able to

identify every last scent exactly, but paying a certain attention to the aromas in the wine glass will increase the enjoyment to be had from an already pleasant experience. It will give us additional information about a wine's quality, which can help in forming an opinion as to whether it pleases us and if it is worth the money we paid for it.

Weighty commercial decisions involving thousands of gallons of wine do not weigh upon us when we are buying a bottle or two for dinner, and consequently we do not have to be as exacting in our judgment of a wine's aroma as the professionals. If we use but two simple criteria we can learn enough about a wine to reach intelligent conclusions about its quality.

To begin, pour your wine into a wine glass, filling it only about a quarter full; any more than that and you risk sloshing it on yourself as you swirl it around in the glass (you can always pour yourself more wine after you've taken a taste of it). Leaving the glass on the table, hold it by its stem and move it in small circles clockwise or counterclockwise; you can move it in whichever direction is easiest for you without affecting the result, but counterclockwise circles tend to be easiest for right-handed people to manage. It may take a while to get the hang of getting the wine to ride up the sides of the glass; once you've got it down you can try picking up the glass to swirl it, which can be a little trickier. The reason for all these gymnastics is that swirling helps release the aroma in the wine. Its aromatic parts are fairly volatile and the swirling in effect knocks them out of the liquid and into the air where they can be inhaled by the nose. (As a test, pour another glass of wine and try inhaling the aroma before swirling and then again after swirling it—the difference will be striking.) Next, tilt the wine glass to your nose and inhale, gently but deeply. You'll be looking for the following things:

The intensity of the aroma. There are four grades of intensity, each largely self-explanatory—*weak, medium, aromatic,* and *very aromatic.*

The quality of the aroma. There are six words that describe the quality—*elegant, ordinary, agreeable, disagreeable, complex,* and *simple.* (These are not listed in any increasing or decreasing order.)

These two aspects will tell you a lot about the character of the wine; in general, a wine's aroma should be a preview of what its taste will be like. A wine with an aroma that is weak and simple will most likely be weak and simple to the taste. A wine can have any combination of intensity and quality; you may come across one with a very aromatic aroma that practically leaps out of the glass at you but is only ordinary in quality, or one that is only medium in intensity but of great complexity. (If you should happen upon a wine that is very aromatic and disagreeable, well, you have my sympathies.)

If you wish, you can consider a third criterion:

The character of the aroma. This is where you come to all those elaborate descriptions of a wine's smell. If a wine's aroma is simple there may be only one or two scents that are noticeable; a complex aroma may contain a half-dozen or more scents, some stronger than others. If you can identify a particular scent, great. But if you have some difficulty with this, you might find it easier to simply name the type of scent you are picking up. Here is a list of some of the major categories that are commonly found in wine with a sampling of the specific scents that they include.

Fruity. In white wines this can include such scents as lemon, pear, and apple; in reds, raspberry, cherry, and banana.

Floral. Rose, violet, and hawthorn in both white and red wines.

Vegetal. Green pepper, eucalyptus, and freshly mown hay in red wines.

Spicy. Black pepper, thyme, clove, and cinnamon, mostly in red wines.

Earthy. Mushroom, truffle, and fallen leaves in older red wines.

Animal. Musk and leather in red wines.

Nutty. Walnut, hazelnut, and toasted almond in white wines.

There are numerous other aromas that don't easily fit into any of the above categories (like honey in some mature white wines and coffee and tobacco in older reds), but you should not let this wide assortment scare you off. As mentioned above, should you forgo this level of noseplay your enjoyment of wines will not be hampered. But if you do decide to pay attention to the aromas and as your experience with wines grows, you will find that what was at first an indiscriminate jumble that only smelled like "wine" will sort itself out into discrete elements, and with time those elements will take on characters distinctive enough to be given names. This takes practice, however, and above that a certain amount of training: you will have to reacquaint yourself with the smells of things and consciously commit these to

CHEERS! ⸻

Although different people will pick out different aromas in different wines, the aromas are certainly there awaiting your discovery. With practice you will eventually be able to define their different characters. To illustrate the fact that there *are* different aromas to be found, try comparing the smells of a white wine called Gewurztraminer from the Alsace region of France with the aroma of another white wine, a Fumé Blanc from California.

Gewurztraminer, Trimbach

If this is your first time concentrating on a wine's aroma, don't worry too much about trying to correctly identify the nature of what you smell; if you feel a little more confident, try to put a name to the impressions you receive using the descriptive terms given on page 43.

1989
Napa Valley
FUMÉ BLANC
Dry Sauvignon Blanc
ALCOHOL 13.5% BY VOLUME

PRODUCED AND BOTTLED BY
ROBERT MONDAVI WINERY
OAKVILLE, CALIFORNIA

Fumé Blanc, Robert Mondavi

memory so they will be there for you when you go reaching for a name to put to an aroma that you may come across in a wine. Get used to stopping at the florist's and smelling the flowers, taking in the scent of fresh fruits and vegetables as you cook, and putting your nose into the jars on your kitchen spice rack. In effect, plug yourself back into the world around you.

Of course, you can forgo all of this and still enjoy your glass of wine. Always remember that cataloging the aromas in a wine is no more crucial to its simple enjoyment than identifying all the scents in a woman's perfume to be able to compliment her on it.

6

The Look of Wine

Of the three basic ways that we can judge a wine—taste, smell, and sight—it is the last of this trio that is the simplest to consider. After all, even people who have never tasted wine before can tell if they are drinking a white or a red with just a glance in the glass. But beyond its color, the visual appearance of a wine can give us clues about its quality, taste, and how it was made—first impressions that are usually confirmed by the nose and then in the mouth.

In speaking of a wine's color, we generally refer to white wines and red wines. In reality, white wine is not really white (like milk, for example), and red wine is not exactly red. When grapes are pressed for white wine, the juice is actually a greenish shade of yellow. The green tinge comes from chlorophyll in the grapes and is the sign of a young wine. With time, the chlorophyll will dissipate and the greenish-yellow can turn to a straw color; if it is capable of aging, a white wine in its maturity may take on a rich golden hue. With red wines, the color can be quite purple in youth, and with time will evolve to include increasing tones of brown.

These changes of color are the result of the wine's inter-action with oxygen. The greater a wine's exposure to air, the quicker the color will shift toward warmer shades of the spectrum—golden in whites and brown in reds.

Now this is all well and good, but what is so important about any of it? It certainly doesn't have much to do with our choice of a wine—people may indicate a preference for a red or a white, but you don't often hear anyone asking for a deep-purple or pale-straw colored wine.

What makes a wine's color so important is that it can serve as a kind of visual quality control to indicate how well a wine has aged. Imagine a loaf of bread whose package is dated to show that it should be fresh for another couple of days, but is already showing signs of mold. You would be justified in thinking that somewhere along the way from the bakery to you this bread was made, handled, or stored im-properly, regardless of the date on the package.

Similarly, a one-year-old wine would be suspect if it exhibited the brown tones of a mature wine much older than the year on its label would indicate. Such a circumstance would suggest that somewhere along the way from the vine-yard to you the wine in that bottle was not handled properly, causing it to take on such an uncharacteristic color.

This can be a first sign of a problem with the wine that

might well be confirmed by an off-aroma in the nose and an unpleasant taste in the mouth. For just as the wine's aroma is a precursor of what can be expected in its taste, so the visual appearance can forecast other aspects of its quality.

In the same way, if a wine exhibits the color of youth even though it may be quite old according to the year on the bottle, the visual signs suggest that it has not yet reached its full maturity and can still develop with time. This is not a fault, but a plus—remember that the longer it takes for a wine to reach maturity, the better it will most likely be. So if you've enjoyed the basic character of such a wine in a restaurant or at home, you might consider buying a few bottles to put away for a couple of years, in the expectation that it will continue to improve and eventually provide you with even greater satisfaction.

The color of a wine is usually closely tied to the type of aromas it will possess, which is only to be expected since both of these aspects are a function of the wine's maturity. Thus, a red wine that shows the deep purple color of youth may be quite fruity in its aroma; a wine with the brick and mahogany tones of maturity may tend to have more complex aromas on the spicy and earthy side. A young white wine still greenish- or pale-yellow can often have simple flowery or grassy aromas, but a white wine capable of aging to the degree of developing a rich, golden color can have an aroma full of more highly developed scents.

There is also one other thing that the color of a wine can tell us—whether it is dry or sweet. This applies to white wines only, since red wines are practically always made in a dry style. The rule of thumb is that the more deeply golden the color, the sweeter the wine will be. And since sweet white wines are capable of long aging, these wines can start out with a bright golden color (which would ordinarily be a sign of maturity in a dry white wine) and evolve from there into shades of rich, deep amber, indicating the developing complexity of character.

The intensity and depth of a wine's color can also be important in indicating quality. Although the type of grape used can be influential here, a deeper, more intense color is generally indicative of a fuller-bodied flavor and a better-quality wine. This is particularly true in reds.

Lighter color in a red wine can be a sign that the grapes from which it was made were rotten or not fully ripe at harvest. Stretching a vineyard's yield (growing a ton of grapes in an area that should only produce a half-ton) will have the same lightening effect on a wine's color by diluting the crop's overall strength of character.

Much of our enjoyment of a wine comes from the anticipatory factor that its appearance creates. It's the same with the food we eat: a plate with meat, vegetables, and potatoes piled on in any old way will tend to be less appetizing than a dish that is attractively presented. Cooks understand that we eat with our eyes as well as with our mouths, and so make an effort to present food in an appealing way. Winemakers also take pains to ensure that the wine we pour into our glasses is attractive to the eye, with a good, clean color and a bright, clear appearance. There should be no cloudiness or solid matter floating in the wine or on its surface; such flotsam and jetsam can be a bad sign, indications of careless winemaking that could be the source of other problems in the wine's aroma and taste.

Because of the importance of its visual inspection, it has become common practice to serve wine in a clear, stemmed glass. Opaque or tinted glass would prevent an unobstructed view of the wine, and the stem gives you some place to hold the glass where your hand won't get in the way. Occasionally, people will have a different-shaped glass for different kinds of wine, but this is not absolutely necessary. A good, all-purpose wine glass approximating the shape illustrated below should meet virtually all of your needs.

Of course, if you are having a picnic in your back yard or are out in the country, don't worry if you opt not to use stemware. Under such circumstances feel free to use paper cups, empty jelly jars sporting pictures of Fred and Wilma Flintstone, or anything else that will serve to carry the wine to your lips in a reasonable fashion. Remember, it wasn't so long ago that people used to drink wine from sheep bladders, so you can't help but be positively swank in comparison.

Once you begin to notice the color of the wine in your glass, you'll see that the variety available in the basic categories of white and red is really quite impressive.

The range of white wine shades is nicely illustrated by the color of a white wine like a California Sauvignon Blanc in

Sauvignon Blanc, Markham

contrast with that of a sweet wine like a Sauternes from France. Of course, the tastes of the two wines will be quite different, a fact that is hinted at by their color (remember, the sweeter a wine, the more golden its hue).

For red wines, compare the purple tones of an Italian Dolcetto with the warmer shading in a French Châteauneuf-du-Pape.

While you are drinking these wines, both whites and reds, try to keep in mind how their overall tastes match their colors—the richer the white wine, the richer its color; the warmer the red wine, the warmer its color.

Sauternes, Château Clos Haut-Peyraguey

PRODUCT OF ITALY

VILLADORIA

DRY RED WINE

Dolcetto d'Alba

DENOMINAZIONE DI ORIGINE CONTROLLATA

Bottled by CE.DI.VI. - Serralunga d'Alba (Italy)
Imported by: AMERICAN B.D. COMPANY
Hawthorne New Jersey - N. J.

Net contents 750 ml.   ✳✳✳✳✳✳   Alcohol 12 % by vol.

Dolcetto d'Alba, Villadoria

MIS EN BOUTEILLE DU CHATEAU

Château de Beaucastel

CHATEAUNEUF-DU-PAPE
APPELLATION CHATEAUNEUF-DU-PAPE CONTROLÉE

Sté FERMIÈRE DES VIGNOBLES PIERRE PERRIN
AU CHATEAU DE BEAUCASTEL COURTHEZON (Vse) FRANCE
PRODUCE
OF
FRANCE
750 ml
ALC. 13.5% BY VOL.
IMPORTED BY Vineyard Brands, Inc. CHESTER, VT
SHIPPED BY ROBERT HAAS SELECTIONS, FRANCE

Châteauneuf-du-Pape, Château de Beaucastel

7

How Wine is Made— The Basics

So now we have a general understanding of what a wine can offer once it is in the glass and in our mouths, but how does it get that way? Well, it all starts with grapes. Wine can be made from a variety of fruits, but for our purposes we will forgo the elderberry, plum, apple, and other folk wines that are out there and focus our attention exclusively on wine made from grapes.

Grapes grow on grapevines, and a collection of grapevines is called a vineyard. Not all types of grape are suitable for making wine and not all kinds of land are suitable for planting vineyards. With very few exceptions, grapes that are good for eating are poor candidates for winemaking and vice versa. (So forget about going down to the supermarket to get the raw material for making your own wine at home.) And land that is good for growing corn, apples, or other crops is generally unsuitable for planting wine grapes.

There is an old saying that to grow grapes for making a good wine the grapevine must suffer. What this means is that vineyards whose grapes are used for wine are usually planted in poor soil that is generally unsuitable for any other purpose; the grapevine must struggle for every bit of nutrient and water it can get. Why does this produce a better grape (which in turn produces a better wine)?

Grapes are composed of water and other substances that get there through the stalk, which is attached to the vine, which is rooted in the soil from which all that water and other substances come. Now if you plant a vine in rich soil with plenty of available water, the plant will not develop an extensive root system—it won't have to since everything it needs for nourishment is readily available. While this may be just comfy for the vine, it's bad for the quality of the grapes. It's like laying around in bed all day on satin sheets, eating bonbons and reading *Photoplay* magazine—sure, you'd love it, but obesity, lack of exercise, and the absence of any intellectual stimulus would soon make you good for nothing.

If the grapevine must actively search for water and nutrients, it will send out a more extensive root system; some very old vines have roots going down as far as 45 feet below the surface. The advantage of this is that the roots have much more surface area in contact with the soil and therefore much more opportunity for nutrients to pass through the vine into the grapes it produces. The more of these sub-stances that pass into the grapes, the more character those grapes will develop; and as might be expected, the greater the character in the grapes, the greater the character in the wine that is made from them.

Above ground the grapevine nourishes itself through photosynthesis, as the plant's leaves transform sunlight into food that is transferred into the grapes, ripening them.

Ripeness in a wine grape can be measured in several ways, but it is important to keep in mind that the grape is a fruit, and like any fruit one of the chief criteria for judging its ripeness is sweetness. As the grapes on the vine ripen, their sugar content increases; when they become fully ripe they are harvested and taken to the winery, where they are pressed to release their juice.

In days past pressing was done by workers who trod the grapes with their feet; today it is done by machines that do the same job more efficiently. If white wine is being made, the juice is allowed to drain away from the skins of the pressed grapes and drip into a separate vat. For red wine the juice is kept in contact with the pressed grapes for periods of up to several weeks. This is because most grapes produce a colorless juice, and it is only through prolonged contact with the red skins of the pressed grapes that their color leaches out into the juice to give it its characteristic hue. (In addition, as we mentioned in Chapter 4, it is in the skin that a good deal of the grape's tannin is found, and this, too, is incorpo-rated into the juice at this stage.)

It is at this point that the process central to turning grape juice into wine occurs—fermentation. Were it not for this, all we'd be left with is deciding whether Château Welch's or Smucker's Grand Cru would go best with the filet mignon for dinner.

Fermentation happens because of the yeast cells on the skins of the grapes. Yeast is a one-celled organism that is found naturally in the environment (which explains its presence on the grapes), and, most important, is responsible for turning sugar into alcohol. This is how it works:

When the grapes are crushed, the yeast on the grape skins is washed off into the juice. Enzymes in the yeast go to work consuming the sugar in the juice, creating by-products of carbon dioxide gas (which escapes into the atmosphere) and alcohol (which remains in the liquid). The more sugar in the juice for the yeast to feast on, the higher the alcohol level in the finished wine. So you can see why it is important for the winemaker to have grapes that are as ripe (sweet) as possible. The quality of the grapes has a direct effect on the quality of the wine.

Although occasionally this process will be stopped by the winemaker before all the sugar has been consumed by the yeast in order to create a wine of greater than normal sweetness, eventually the yeast will run out of sugar to feed on and dies; sometimes the yeast will create so much alcohol that, in effect, it changes the balance in its environment and can no longer survive. (This generally happens when the alcohol level reaches 15 percent.) In any event, fermentation will automatically stop. The dead yeast cells are removed from the wine (for now it is wine and no longer grape juice) and it can be bottled and drunk.

Up to this point everything that is called wine undergoes this same basic process: grapes, juice, fermentation, wine. At every step of the way, however, from planting the grapevines to deciding when to sell the wine, the winemaker has options that help determine what the character, quality, and taste of the finished product will be. We'll look at some of these now.

8

How Wine is Made—The Manufacturer's Options

In theory, you can use anything to hold the wine after fermentation, and winemakers employ various types of containers of differing sizes and materials.

Stainless steel tanks are popular and practical: they are easy to clean and can be used again and again. Many wineries use concrete vats lined with epoxy for the same reasons. Both of these materials are perfectly adequate for holding a wine while it waits to be bottled. These materials, however, are like roadside motels that offer little more than a place to stay. There are no monogrammed towels, no picture postcards or letterhead in the desk drawer, no cellophane-wrapped toothbrushes with the name of the establishment on it, nothing to take away to show that you were ever there. Wine that is held in stainless steel or concrete comes away from the encounter with nothing to show for it; it doesn't acquire a taste of steel or a hint of concrete in its aroma. (Good thing, too.) These materials don't hurt the wine, but they don't add anything at all.

If stainless steel is a motel, then oak is a luxury hotel. Wine that has stayed in oak for a prolonged period can be very much changed by the experience, generally for the better. In addition to whatever qualities of its own the wine may possess, oak adds its own influence to the final character. And because wood is a porous material, oak barrels also allow oxygen to reach the wine inside in a limited and controlled manner that helps it to mature. The result is a taste that is more complex, and as we've already said, the more a wine is able to keep your palate interested the better it is—otherwise you might as well be drinking water.

Unfortunately, just as the Ritz is more expensive than Motel 6, so oak costs more than stainless steel or concrete. The life of an oak barrel is generally four years; after that just about everything that it has to contribute to a wine's character has already been extracted and it has nothing left to give. Worse, an old barrel can begin to decay and transmit off-tastes and unpleasant aromas to the wine. If a winemaker chooses to put a wine in used barrels, these are generally no more than three years old.

Having ascertained that putting wine into oak barrels can be a good thing, should every wine go into oak and how long is sufficient? The answer: it depends. Not all wines have enough character to stand up to having such luxury lavished on them, and the result can be similar to what may happen with people: they can be spoiled.

From a winemaking point of view, whether or not a wine should "see" oak (as the expression goes), and for what length of time, depends on the type of grapes that were used, the quality of the wine going into the barrels, and the character of the wine that the winemaker wants to end up with.

Not all grape varieties make a wine of sufficient potential to profit from the benefits that oak can provide. Putting such a minor wine in oak barrels would be like giving a weekend softball team the Astrodome to play in. Sure, it would give the players a feeling of class, but they couldn't fill all the seats in the stadium and they'd hit far fewer home runs than they would in more appropriate surroundings. The experience would be wastefully extravagant and the results simply disappointing.

Similarly, some wine, even when made from a better variety of grapes, does not possess enough personality to stand up to prolonged aging in oak. It may be that the land in which the grapevines were planted was not ideally suited for the purpose of producing a fine wine or the weather did not cooperate to fully ripen the grapes. Whatever character such a wine did possess would be overpowered by the contribution made by the barrels so that the end result would be less a product of the grapevine than the oak tree. In such a case, a winemaker may decide to keep the wine in oak for only a year or two instead of three or four, or else to work with used barrels that have already given up the most potent part of their character to a previous wine.

But if a young wine is very powerful and possesses sufficient quality in its own right, then a prolonged time in new oak barrels can result in a wine whose virtues are amplified. In general, it is only the finest wines that can sustain such treatment, and then not every maker of fine wine will opt for it; it's all a question of how strong an oak character the winemaker decides the wine should have.

In general, however, the longer a wine is allowed to remain in the barrel, the better the result, if only because of the beneficial effects of oxidation that occur as air passes through the wood to the wine. The effects of this controlled exposure to air is also known as barrel aging. The result of such treatment is that tannins are mellowed, discrete elements in the wine are more harmoniously knit together, and by being held at the winery, the wine is able to begin maturing under more favorable and stable conditions than might otherwise be available sitting on the shelf in a wine store or by the steam pipes in your closet.

Under some circumstances, wines held at the winery in oak barrels may have the word "reserve" on the label. At its best, this can be a sign of quality, indicating that the wine so designated is more ready for drinking than another that has been bottled directly after fermentation. Glass bottles, like stainless steel tanks, are inert containers and do not effect any change in the wine that they hold. Although these wines may experience bottle aging depending on how long they remain in glass, they will not have any of the complexity that oak aging can impart.

But the term "reserve" is not always regulated by law or professional practice, and so can mean little more than that instead of putting the wine on the market immediately after fermentation, the winemaker decided to wait an extra month; obviously, the wine that is the result of such a practice will have none of the benefits of aging that the word "reserve" on the label would indicate.

Another matter affecting the quality of the finished wine is whether one individual chooses to undertake the wine-making process from beginning to end. Throughout this book we have referred to the winemaker as the person responsible for everything from growing the grapes to bottling the wine. Although this is the case much of the time, not all wine is made in this way.

There are a number of reasons why more than just one person may be involved in the process. The grape grower may be excellent at producing fruit of the finest quality, but have neither the talent nor the inclination to make wine from it; thus the grapes are sold to a winemaker who will best be able to bring them to their full potential. Or the grower will actually make the wine and see it through its fermentation, but be unable to properly care for it until it's ready for bottling or be unwilling to tie up a significant amount of money in it until it's ready for sale. In this case the young wine will be sold to someone else who has the oak barrels, the cellar space, or the money necessary to bring the wine to maturity.

The laws controlling wine production do not require that one individual be responsible from beginning to end, and often a collaboration in which each person performs one specific operation, be it growing the grapes, fermenting the juice, or bottling and marketing the finished product, can create a wine of excellent quality. Still, it is generally believed that when one person is in charge of the entire process the result is a greater consistency of quality, and therefore a better wine. So when a winemaker is responsible for both growing the grapes and maturing the wine, the label is entitled to carry the designation "estate bottled" as a sign of the potentially higher quality such winemaking is capable of. Most wine-producing countries have some equivalent term for this, and a list of some of the more commonly encountered ones appears in Appendix A.

The influence of oak in a wine can be one of the more subtle elements in a wine's character. Although the taste of oak may not be readily identifiable (how many of us have taken a

Rioja, Bodegas Montecillo "Viña Cumbrero" Crianza

bite out of the Chippendale to register the taste in our memories), the richness that it imparts can be an easier telltale sign to look for.

Compare a wine like a basic Spanish Rioja with the Gran Reserva version of the same wine.

According to the wine laws of Spain, a basic Rioja will get as little as 12 months' aging in oak casks, while Gran Reserva

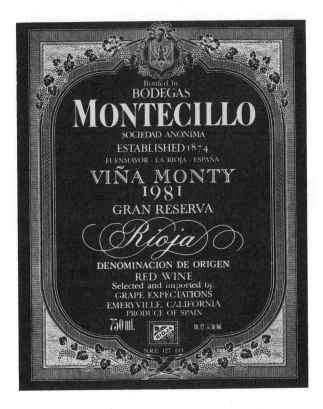

Rioja, Bodegas Montecillo "Viña Monty" Gran Reserva

wines must remain in oak for at least 24 months. The term "reserve" (or *reserva, riserva,* or any other international variant on the word) signifies, among other things, that the wine in question has received an extended aging in oak compared to the basic version of that wine.

Sometimes, however, a wine may receive significant oak aging without any official indication to that effect on the label. It is then reasonable to ask how one is to know if this is the case, short of doing a lot of research and reading. Two methods are readily at hand: first, ask the salesperson where you buy your wine—a good one will be able to tell you the answer, or will have the reference material at hand to get that information for you. Second, and somewhat easier, is to look for a back label on the bottle that gives details of the wine's production. These labels can often be rather elaborate affairs, offering more information about the technical side of winemaking than you may ever wish to know. But given the expense involved in using oak casks, if the wine has spent any time in them at all, that fact will in all likelihood be acknowledged.

9

Pink, Sweet, and Bubbly

The red and white table wines we have been discussing comprise about 90 percent of the average wine drinker's consumption. Now we'll look at three types of wine that make up the other 10 percent.

Rosé wines are made from red wine grapes, but are more like white wines in their character. Still, they are different enough to be neither one nor the other and are considered a distinct type of wine. Rosés are distinguished primarily by their color, which can range over a variety of shades of pink. This color is *not* the result of blending red and white wines (there is one significant exception that we will discuss shortly); in general, rosé wines are made by allowing the colorless juice from red grapes to remain in contact with the grape

CHEERS! ───────────────────

Because rosé wines are not red or white, they are often looked down upon for being neither fish nor fowl. But some good quality can indeed be found in this category.

APPELLATION TAVEL CONTROLÉE

CHÂTEAU D'AQUERIA
TAVEL
ROSÉ

SOCIÉTÉ JEAN OLIVIER, PRODUCTEUR, 30 TAVEL FRANCE

750 ML
(25,4 FL OZ)
TAVEL ROSE
TABLE WINE

KOBRAND
Wines   *Spirits*

PRODUCE
OF FRANCE

IMPORTED BY KOBRAND CORPORATION NEW-YORK N. Y. ALC. BY VOL 13,5 %

Tavel Rosé, Château d'Aqueria

Try a wine from Tavel or Anjou in France to find something ideal for a summer picnic or a simple family meal.

Although the taste of a rosé wine will not be as full as a red wine (remember, the tannin content that gives reds so much of their fullness is minimal here), a good rosé wine should still have a distinctive character, not wishy washy or mediocre— you should get a mouth-filling sensation of pleasing flavor with a reasonably long finish. Just as with any wine.

Rosé d'Anjou, Château de Tigné

skins for a brief period after pressing. As we saw in our discussion of how red wine is made, the pressed juice takes on color and tannin from the skins as they macerate together. But unlike red wines, where the skins can remain in contact with the juice for a period of weeks, rosé wines are made by draining away the juice after just a day or two of contact. In such a limited time the juice is able to extract only a small amount of color and practically no tannin, making it more like a white wine in character. When speaking of the taste of rosés, it is the white wine vocabulary that is used, although their aromas will often have more in common with those of red wines.

The depth of color in a rosé wine depends on the type of grapes used and how long the skins remained in contact with the pressed juice; it is not an index of a wine's quality.

Dessert wines are those that are especially sweet to the taste and are therefore served with the dessert course of a meal. These wines are not sweet because of any sugar added to them during production. Indeed, such adulteration of a dessert wine is illegal and would produce an inferior result in any event. The sweetness of dessert wines comes from how the grapes are handled in the vineyard, not the winery.

We've already noted that a ripe grape will have a rich sugar content, but this alone is not sufficient to make a wine especially sweet. It is necessary to increase the proportion of sugar in the grape relative to its other components. Since the major component in the grape is water, the most effective way of increasing its proportion of sugar is to decrease its proportion of water, and there are two methods that achieve this end.

By leaving the grapes on the vine past their point of maturation, the continued exposure to the heat of the sun will cause the grapes to shrivel and lose water through evaporation. Sometimes the grapes are harvested as usual and the ripe bunches are placed on straw mats where this process of evaporation takes place off the vine. Because only water evaporates and not sugar, the grapes' sweetness is increased. The dehydrated grapes (practically raisins) are pressed, and although the yield is greatly reduced, the liquid that is extracted has a much higher sugar level than normal. (If the growing climate is suitably chilly, the grapes may be left on the vine until the end of autumn so the first frost can freeze them, concentrating their sugar content even further; the sweet wine made from these frozen grapes is called *ice wine.*)

A second method for increasing the sugar content of the grapes is something of a variation on the first method. Under certain climatic conditions, a particular bacteria can develop on the grapes. This bacteria punctures the grapes' skin and evaporation results. The grapes take on a shriveled, rotten appearance that is not at all indicative of the superior quality of the sweet wine that it makes. This bacteria is referred to as "noble rot" and is much sought after in the making of dessert wines (as opposed to other types of rot, which attack not just the skin but the entire grape and can destroy its quality completely). In addition to promoting dehydration in the grapes, the bacteria also adds to the taste of the wine through its incorporation into the juice of the pressed grapes. It is the added character contributed by the bacteria that gives wines made from nobly rotten grapes an

C H E E R S ! ─────────────

Sweet wines are unmistakably sweet, which is why they are often called dessert wines. A glass of one of these can make a suitable end to a meal on its own. Because these are too rich to be drunk in amounts typical for drier wines, sweet

Sauternes, Château d'Arche

wines are widely available in half-bottle size, which are large enough to satisfy the needs of four to six people.

Try a Sauternes from France made from nobly rotted grapes or a late-harvest wine from New York State whose grapes have overmatured on the vine.

Compare these wines with a White Zinfandel (which was the least dry of the white wines suggested in Chapter 3) and you'll see exactly how great a distance separates sweet from dry.

Johannisberg Riesling—Late Harvest, Hermann J. Wiemer

extra dimension of quality compared to wines made from overmatured grapes.

After the grapes are pressed fermentation takes place. As we've seen in Chapter 7, fermentation involves enzymes in the yeast feeding on the sugar in the grape juice to produce alcohol; in this case, such an abundance of available sugar should easily produce alcohol levels of 20 percent and more. But when the alcohol level approaches 15 percent the yeast can no longer survive, leaving significant amounts of unfermented grape sugar in the finished wine; this is the source of the sweetness in dessert wines.

The color of dessert wines is generally of a deeper yellow than dry white wines, turning to a dark amber as they mature. These wines also have a thicker, more syrupy consistency compared to other wines, reflecting their increased sugar content.

The third type of wine that we'll look at is *sparkling wine*, including the most well-known example of this type, Champagne. Not all sparkling wines are Champagne, since by law only sparkling wines made in the Champagne region of France using the traditional Champagne method can legally use that name. But other wines made elsewhere by the same method can also be of excellent quality.

Sparkling wines differ from all other types by being fermented *twice*. The first fermentation results in a still (nonsparkling) wine just like all the others we've discussed. This wine is pumped into a bottle or tank with a mixture of yeast and sugar to produce a second fermentation.

As we've seen, fermentation produces alcohol and carbon dioxide gas, and during the first fermentation the gas is allowed to escape into the air—the important thing at this stage is to change the grape's sugar into alcohol. The purpose of the second fermentation is to produce more carbon dioxide, this time keeping it in the wine. Since this second fermentation occurs in a closed container, the gas stays trapped in the liquid, giving sparkling wine its sparkle.

Getting the bubbles in a sparkling wine is easy; the trick is in removing the dead yeast cells from the wine after the second fermentation to obtain a clear, clean wine. There are three methods that are commonly used to achieve this, and the method used plays a large part in determining the quality and the cost of the finished wine.

In the Champagne method mentioned above, the wine undergoes its second fermentation in the same bottle in which it is sold to you. Removing the yeast is a fairly involved process in which the bottles are jiggled over a period of weeks to move the yeast into the neck where it can be more easily collected and removed. This is a labor-intensive, time-consuming process that contributes greatly to the final cost—it also produces the best-quality sparkling wine. Those that are made by this method will have the words "Champagne method" or "traditional method" on the label (or, of course, "Champagne" if it is made in the Champagne region of France).

Similar to this is the transfer method, in which the wine has its second fermentation in a bottle, but is then emptied into a tank where the yeast is filtered out before the wine is pumped back into another bottle. The label on these wines may read "naturally fermented in the bottle," although it would be less ambiguous to say "naturally fermented in *a* bottle," since the bottle referred to is not the one that's in your hands.

The simplest, cheapest, and least quality-conscious way of removing the yeast is the bulk method. Here the wine undergoes its second fermentation in bulk inside a large, sealed tank; it is then a simple matter to filter out the yeast as it is finally put into bottles.

The last two methods produce a sparkling wine whose bubbles are larger and dissipate more rapidly than those made by the Champagne method. And when it comes to sparkling wine what you're paying for is the bubbles, so the longer they last, the more you're getting for your money.

Regardless of the method used, a sparkling wine can be either vintage or nonvintage. As with still wine, if there is a vintage on the bottle it means that all the grapes used to make the wine were harvested in that year. In the Champagne region, the climate is so hard on the grapes that it is only in years of better-than-average weather that a vintage wine is made. Otherwise the usual practice is to blend reserve wines from several years before starting the second fermentation. Great care and skill are used in blending these wines in order to consistently arrive at the "house style" that is the distinguishing mark of each Champagne producer.

There is also rosé sparkling wine which, like rosé wine without the bubbles, is pink in color. But unlike the still wine that gets its color from letting the grape juice stay in contact with the red grape skins for a brief period, rosé sparkling wines are made by actually blending red and white wines. Because of the poor quality of so much of the "pink champagne" that is common on the American market, this type of wine is generally not taken as seriously as it deserves. A fine rosé Champagne can in fact be a superior wine, as reflected by the higher price it commands in the wine shop and on wine lists in restaurants.

Just before the mushroom-shaped cork is finally squeezed into the bottle to seal it, a second dose of sugar is added to the wine. Since most sparkling wines are naturally very acidic in taste, the final addition of sugar is intended to give the wine a balance that will make it more appealing. The amount of sugar added can vary, and a single winemaker can produce a whole range of sparkling wines of differing sweetness. From driest to sweetest, the terms on the label that describe a sparkling wine are: *natural* (a specialty wine with no sugar added), *brut* (this is the driest and most popular type generally available), *extra dry* (which, despite its name, is sweeter than brut), *sec* (or *seco*, a fairly sweet type), *demi-sec* (quite sweet), and *doux* (or *dulce*, a very sweet specialty variety that is seldom found in America).

Champagne tends to be pretty pricey because of all the labor that goes into its production and the image of luxury that it conveys. But there are other sparkling wines made in France and elsewhere, more moderately priced, that can be just as pleasant for an office party toast or to give a special feeling to a quiet dinner at home.

Compare a French Champagne with a sparkling wine from another region of France. (Remember, because the wine is not made in the Champagne region, French wine laws do

Champagne, Bollinger

not allow it to call itself Champagne, even if all the other aspects of its production are the same.)

Beginning in the 1970s, many Champagne companies began establishing vineyards in California to make sparkling wines using the same techniques as in France. Compare one of these company's Champagnes with the sparkling wine it makes in California (which will always be less expensive) to see if any difference in taste is worth the difference in price to you.

French Sparkling Wine, Bouvet

Other countries, such as Spain, also make sparkling wines of fine quality that are extremely good values.

At such prices there's no reason why you shouldn't drink a sparkling wine at least once a week, if only to celebrate having made it to Friday.

Champagne, Taittinger

California Sparkling Wine, Domaine Carneros

Spanish Sparkling Wine—Cava, Freixenet

10

How Wine is Packaged

Regardless of how the winemaker decides to treat the wine, sooner or later it's going to be packaged. (I've deliberately avoided the word "bottled" since not all wine gets put into glass containers.) Packaging is an important stage in a wine's production, and several methods are commonly used. Regardless of its shape or composition, however, every type of container has two basic functions: to transport the wine from the winery to your glass, and to ensure that there is no loss in quality along the way. The decision regarding which method to use is made by the winemaker according to how and to whom the wine is to be sold.

For most winemakers and wine drinkers, the container of choice is the glass bottle, closed with a cork stopper. This combination has been in use for three centuries, and for the past 200 years its basic form has changed relatively little. This continuity in its design has given the wine bottle an association with its contents that is practically indissoluble and virtually unmatched by any other combination of package and product. For many people, a cork and bottle are the defining characteristics of a fine wine.

But as inevitably perfect as the cork and bottle may seem, this was simply an evolutionary development in a continuing process by winemakers to more efficiently package their wine, not the culmination of a search for the ideal container. At a certain point in the seventeenth century the manufacture of glass bottles became cheap and cork was rediscovered to be suitable for use as a stopper; the rest is history.

All things considered, the glass bottle is a reasonably good container. It is inexpensive, not prone to leaks (although breakage can be a problem), and an inert material that will not interact with the wine in any way. This provides a clean, stable, airtight environment in which a wine's various components can pull themselves together in the process called bottle aging (as opposed to barrel aging, which was discussed in Chapter 8). In this regard, the glass bottle is an almost perfect container. Almost. The major weakness with the cork and bottle is not with the glass bottle itself, but with the cork stopper.

If there is an imperfection in the glass it will make itself known through breakage, a highly visible means of indicating that something is wrong. The cork, however, may develop imperfections that can have a detrimental effect on the wine that often remains undetected until after the wine is purchased. Bacteria in the cork or chemical compounds inadvertently created during its manufacture can pass into the wine to spoil its taste and aroma. No one is sure why this happens or how to prevent it, and some estimates have indicated that bad corks may be responsible for spoiling as many as six bottles out of every 100. (In all fairness, this is not a lot—unless you happen to have one of the six bad bottles.)

There does exist an effective solution to this problem, but few people care to give it serious consideration: the screw-top cap. Yes, that's right, the same screw-top that has been around for ages on all those high-alcohol, low-quality wines. If the cork indicates quality in a wine, then the screw-top is a sign of an utter lack of class, right?

It is ironic that the wines that are least in need of the more exacting protection that the screw-top offers are the very ones to receive it, while the wines that would benefit most from it shun the screw-top like the plague because of the dubious company it has kept. Winemakers acknowledge the superiority of the screw-top but because of the general perception among wine drinkers that only a bottle with a cork can contain a fine wine, we are stuck with a seventeenth-century method when a superior twentieth-century solution exists.

Another nontraditional method of packaging wine is the descriptively named "bag-in-a-box," a plastic-lined foil bag filled with wine that is sealed in a cardboard box. This type of container has been around since the 1970s, and for many wines is actually superior to the traditional cork-and-bottle package.

The chief advantage of the bag-in-a-box is the fact that the wine is inside a closed system: when the spigot in the side of the bag is opened, the wine pours out and the foil bag collapses as it empties. No air comes into the bag or in contact with the unpoured wine, so what remains stays free from the oxidizing effects of the air that can spoil so many wines left in half-full bottles; wine in a partially filled bag-in-a-box can remain drinkable for almost a year, as opposed to only a few days in a recorked bottle. The only problem with the bag-in-a-box is, once again, one of image; regardless of how well-suited it is for the serving of wine, it has not gained the popularity it merits. After all, no famous (and expensive) wines come in a box, therefore how good can it be?

Well, unlike the screw-top cap, the bag-in-a-box is not intended for all wines—better wines that can improve with age would not be best served by this method of packaging. While the screw-top cap will not interfere with bottle aging (in fact, it may improve the chances for successful aging by preventing oxidation or other alteration more successfully than cork), the bag-in-a-box is better suited for wines that are made for current consumption, the type of wine you pick up on the way home to have with dinner that evening.

The bag-in-a-box is perhaps best suited for serving wine at picnics or other outdoor events where there is a danger of breakage in carrying glass bottles. The box is not as easy to knock over as a bottle, is lighter to carry, and the ease of pouring is also a plus—the spigot is as easy to use as the cold-water tap on the kitchen sink. Also, when refrigerated ahead of time, the foil bag will keep the wine inside it

Just as there are wines that are felt to be more appropriate for certain occasions (Champagne with celebrations, for instance), so are there wine containers that are likely to be favored in particular circumstances.

Large glass bottles, or jugs, are traditional favorites for picnics, parties, and other informal get-togethers. The wines that are packaged in these big sizes are ideally suited for such gatherings, being good, basic, easy-drinking beverages that don't seek to be the focal point of the social event. And buying one big bottle instead of several smaller ones has the

Chenin Blanc, Almaden

same convenience as purchasing the giant-size packages of other foods for the occasion.

This is the province of the large producers, whose names are fairly well known: Almaden, Gallo, Paul Masson, and others. These wines are made in great quantities for wide availability, so consistency is of prime importance—you won't find vintage years on these wine labels or the variation in the wine's character that this can entail. And since they represent good value for your money, jug wines are perfect for everyday drinking, too.

Much of what has been said for the jug container can apply to the bag-in-a-box as well, and many of the wines that come in large bottles are available in this format too.

California Burgundy, Paul Masson

cold for several hours, which is great for serving white wines (or even fruity young reds) on hot summer days. Happily, some pretty good wines are available in the bag-in-a-box, and these packages are usually larger than the standard 750 ml bottle, so it can also be an economical way to purchase as well.

The point of all this is that the packaging should not be the determining factor in deciding on the quality of a wine, which it all too often is. As we have seen in the question of the cork versus the screw-top, both experienced and occasional wine drinkers are all too often taken in by the trappings. Keep in mind the cardinal rule: what is important about a wine is its taste, and anything that helps to preserve the quality of that taste should not necessarily be rejected because of popular opinion.

11

The Wine Label

Much of the trepidation about reading a wine label has nothing at all to do with wine. The main problem for many people is that most wine comes from France, Italy, Germany, Spain, or elsewhere, so there are a lot of words on the label in a language other than English. As Americans, our aversion to foreign languages is legendary, and in our best of all possible worlds the only words on a label would be those that simply stated what type of wine was in the bottle. But because of the various laws in each of the wine-producing countries throughout the world additional information is mandatory, making the whole business of understanding a label appear complicated enough to turn people away from wine altogether. As paradoxical as it may seem, however, all these various laws actually make reading a wine label much simpler than it might otherwise be.

Wine laws are designed to control every aspect of winemaking from the grapes on up. The purpose of all these rules is twofold: first, to protect the conscientious winemakers by ensuring that their region's reputation as a source of fine wine is not undermined by the poor practices of an unscrupulous few, be they fellow winemakers tempted to take shortcuts in their production methods, or anyone who might handle a wine as it passes along the chain of distribution; and second, to protect you, the wine buyer, by guaranteeing that the basic quality and character to be expected from a given type of wine will indeed be there.

Each wine-producing country has its own set of laws that are tailored to meet the specific needs of its national wine industry. But since the basic principles of winemaking are the same regardless of where a wine is made, many countries have opted to forgo reinventing the wheel and have simply modeled their regulations on those formulated by the French in 1935, the first comprehensive and effective wine laws in modern times. Although there are variations in many of the agricultural aspects of these laws, the regulations controlling labeling are actually quite consistent from country to country and serve to restrict what may appear on the label to a fairly standard set of information.

In addition, the U.S. government has its own set of regulations for what information must appear on wines imported from abroad, and keeping in mind its citizens' aversion to foreign languages, these laws specify that this additional information must appear in English.

Thus, regardless of where a wine comes from, there will always be certain standard information on every label. Each item may be in a different place from label to label, but it will definitely be somewhere. Other information is optional, not mandatory, but it appears frequently enough to merit inclusion in the following list of what you will generally find on a wine label:

1. The name of the wine—mandatory.
2. The name of the producer—mandatory.
3. The name and location of the person or company legally responsible for making the wine (in some cases this name can be the same as #2)—mandatory.
4. The volume of the bottle's contents (this can appear either on the label itself or molded into the glass bottle, usually near its base)—mandatory.
5. The alcohol content of the wine (this is usually expressed as a percentage of the wine's volume)—mandatory.
6. The name of the shipper and importer responsible for bringing the wine to the United States (occasionally the shipper and importer are two different companies)—mandatory.
7. The country of origin (always in English)—mandatory.
8. The kind of wine (always in English)—optional.
9. The quality of the wine—optional.
10. The year the wine was made, also known as the vintage—optional.

Let's look at each of these in a little more detail to see why it is thought to be important enough to put on the label.

The name of the wine. This is almost self-evident. The name is the first thing that you look for because it defines in the broadest terms what type of wine is in that bottle and what kind of taste, character, and style it will have. Just as when you go grocery shopping you will first look for a type of food (e.g., tomato paste, creamed corn, applesauce, etc.), with wine you will first look for the basic type. This is usually defined by the place where the wine comes from (Bordeaux or Rioja, for instance), or the predominant variety of grape used (like chardonnay or cabernet sauvignon). This information may not appear in the largest print on the label, but nevertheless, it is of prime importance.

The name of the producer. This is, in effect, the brand name of the wine; as a result, this will usually be the most prominently displayed information on the label. Just as there are numerous makers of applesauce or creamed corn, so there are numerous producers of Bordeaux or Rioja wines. While the basic type of wine will have a certain recognizably standard character, each producer's will have a slightly different style based on the winemaker's personal preferences; this serves to distinguish that wine from others of the same type in the hope of keeping you coming back to that one for more—brand loyalty, in effect.

The name and location of the person or company legally responsible. This may be the same as the name of the producer (as is the case with Coors beer, for instance), or the producer may do business under another name or be part of a larger operation (like Anheuser-Busch, which makes Budweiser beer).

The volume of the bottle. This is self-explanatory.

The alcohol content of the wine. This is similar to the list of ingredients on the label of a can of food, except that here the only ingredient listed is the alcohol. The alcohol content can give you an idea of the strength of the wine and, possibly, the ripeness of the grapes (remember, the riper the grapes, the more sugar they have; the more sugar in the grapes, the more alcohol in the finished wine).

The name of the shipper and importer. This is on the label to give you a more complete picture of who had their hands on the wine at every step of its way to you, from the winemaker to the shipper who brought it from overseas to America, the importer who took it off the boat and stored it in the warehouse here, and the wine store or restaurant where you purchased it.

The country of origin. If nothing else, this will at least tell you the language in which all the other foreign words on the label are written.

The kind of wine. This is the most basic description of the kind of wine in the bottle. Thus if you are faced with a wine with which you are not familiar, you can look here and get a general idea of where it is from and what it may be like.

The quality of the wine. This is the rating that the wine has earned based on the wine laws of the country in which it was made. This is similar to the way we grade a cut of meat as prime, choice, or standard. (Each country has its own system for designating quality; some of these are outlined in Appendix A.)

The vintage. This will be discussed in detail in Chapter 12.

As stated above, virtually all wine will have this information somewhere on its label. Occasionally, some items will be found separately on what is called a strip label above or beneath the main one or on a back label that is found, as the name implies, on the back of the bottle; this is usually the information required by U.S. regulations such as the importer and alcohol content. There is no difference in quality between a wine that has all this on one label and another that contains a strip or back label—it's simply a business decision. If a wine is imported in large enough quantities, the winemaker or importer may find it practical to have labels specially printed for the American market that contain all of the additionally required information; otherwise, the winemaker will simply use the standard label for the wine and it is up to the shipper or importer to make and add the second label to meet the requirements of the U.S. authorities. (Of course, for wines made in America, information about the shipper and importer does not apply, and the country of origin will be replaced by the wine's state or region of production.)

To give you a better idea of the various forms in which all of this can appear, here is a sampling of wine labels from countries around the world. (A few of the labels may not contain all of the information discussed above; some items, like vintage, may be printed on neck or strip labels that are not shown.)

If you are able to understand the label on a can of peas or a jar of apricot jam in the supermarket, you should have no problem in understanding the label on a bottle of wine. The basic purpose of each is exactly the same and the information that each is required by law to contain is remarkably similar: the name of the type of product in the container, who made it, their address, the container's volume, an expiration date, and the like.

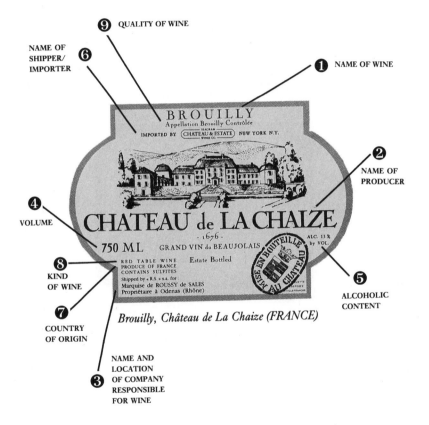

⑨ QUALITY OF WINE

NAME OF SHIPPER/ IMPORTER ⑥

① NAME OF WINE

② NAME OF PRODUCER

④ VOLUME

⑧ KIND OF WINE

⑤ ALCOHOLIC CONTENT

⑦ COUNTRY OF ORIGIN

③ NAME AND LOCATION OF COMPANY RESPONSIBLE FOR WINE

BROUILLY
Appellation Brouilly Contrôlée
— SEAGRAM —
IMPORTED BY (CHATEAU & ESTATE) NEW YORK N.Y.
WINES CO.

CHATEAU de LA CHAIZE
- 1676 -
750 ML   GRAND VIN du BEAUJOLAIS   ALC. 13 % by VOL.

RED TABLE WINE   Estate Bottled
PRODUCE OF FRANCE
CONTAINS SULFITES
Shipped by « R.S. » s.a. for:
Marquise de ROUSSY de SALES
Propriétaire à Odenas (Rhône)

Brouilly, Château de La Chaize (FRANCE)

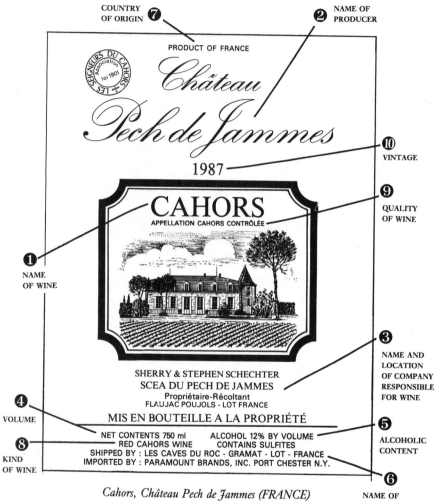

COUNTRY OF ORIGIN **7**

NAME OF PRODUCER **2**

PRODUCT OF FRANCE

Château

Pech de Jammes

1987

10 VINTAGE

CAHORS
APPELLATION CAHORS CONTRÔLÉE

9 QUALITY OF WINE

1 NAME OF WINE

SHERRY & STEPHEN SCHECHTER
SCEA DU PECH DE JAMMES
Propriétaire-Récoltant
FLAUJAC POUJOLS - LOT FRANCE
MIS EN BOUTEILLE A LA PROPRIÉTÉ

3 NAME AND LOCATION OF COMPANY RESPONSIBLE FOR WINE

4 VOLUME

NET CONTENTS 750 ml   ALCOHOL 12% BY VOLUME
RED CAHORS WINE   CONTAINS SULFITES
SHIPPED BY : LES CAVES DU ROC - GRAMAT - LOT - FRANCE
IMPORTED BY : PARAMOUNT BRANDS, INC. PORT CHESTER N.Y.

5 ALCOHOLIC CONTENT

8 KIND OF WINE

6 NAME OF SHIPPER/IMPORTER

Cahors, Château Pech de Jammes (FRANCE)

Barbera d'Alba, Cerequio (ITALY)

Montepulciano d'Abruzzo, Colli del Moro (ITALY)

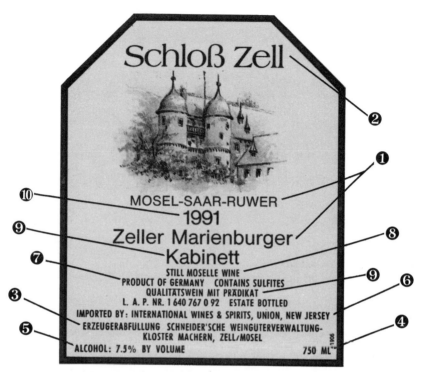

Schloß Zell

❿ **MOSEL-SAAR-RUWER**
❾ **1991**
❶ **Zeller Marienburger** ❽
❼ **Kabinett**
STILL MOSELLE WINE ❾
PRODUCT OF GERMANY   CONTAINS SULFITES ❻
QUALITÄTSWEIN MIT PRÄDIKAT
❸ L. A. P. NR. 1 640 767 0 92   ESTATE BOTTLED
IMPORTED BY: INTERNATIONAL WINES & SPIRITS, UNION, NEW JERSEY ❹
❺ ERZEUGERABFÜLLUNG SCHNEIDER'SCHE WEINGÜTERVERWALTUNG-
KLOSTER MACHERN, ZELL/MOSEL
ALCOHOL: 7.5% BY VOLUME   750 ML

❷ ❶ ❿

Zeller Marienburger Kabinett, Schloss Zell (GERMANY)

ST. CHRISTINA WEINKELLEREI
D-5555 PIESPORT AN DER MOSEL

❷ &
❸

❺
❼ ALC. 7.5 % BY VOL
PRODUCE OF GERMANY   Cont.:750ml ℮ ❹

❶ **1990** ❿
MOSEL-SAAR-RUWER
❽ **Piesporter Michelsberg Spätlese** ❾
WHITE WINE – CONTAINS SULFITES
❾ QUALITÄTSWEIN MIT PRÄDIKAT - A. P. NR. 2 907 668 019 92 ❻
IMPORTED BY: ATLANTIC IMPORTS, INC., SEAFORD, N.Y. 11783
❸ BOTTLED BY: 907 668 IN D-RP 231 105
SHIPPED BY: ST. CHRISTINA WEINKELLEREI GMBH, PIESPORT/GERMANY

Piesporter Michelsberg Spätlese, St. Christina Weinkellerei
(GERMANY)

GUELBENZU

BODEGA DEL JARDIN

1851

② GUELBENZU

⑩ 1989

① **NAVARRA**
Denominación de origen

⑨ NAVARRA

⑧ ⑤ NAVARRA RED WINE - PRODUCT OF SPAIN ⑦ ④

12.5% ALC./VOL.- CONTAINS SULFITES - 750 ML. ⑥

Sole Agents: Classical Wines from Spain-Seattle, WA

③ Embotellado por Bodegas GUELBENZU S.L. R.E. 6936/NA
CASCANTE

Navarra, Guelbenzu (SPAIN)

RED WINE ⑧
PENEDES
Denominación de Origen ①
⑨

② **MONT MARÇAL**

⑩ **TINTO CRIANZA**
③ 1988

Estate-Bottled by
Cavas y Bodegas Manuel Sancho e Hijas, S.A.
Castellví de la Marca, Barcelona, Spain

④ ⑥

RE 5322-

SOLE U.S. AGENTS: CLASSICAL WINES - SEATTLE, WA ⑦
750 ML - 12% ALC./VOL. - CONTAINS SULFITES - PRODUCT OF SPAIN
⑤

Penedes, Mont Marcal (SPAIN)

Chardonnay, Penfolds (AUSTRALIA)

Cabernet Sauvignon, Vasse Felix (AUSTRALIA)

102

Cabernet Sauvignon, Cousiño-Macul (CHILE)

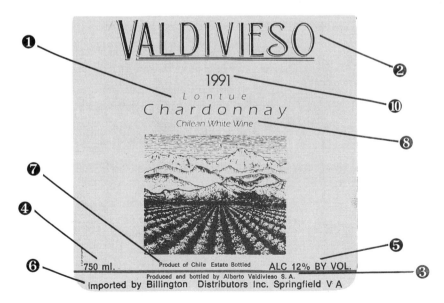

Chardonnay, Valdivieso (CHILE)

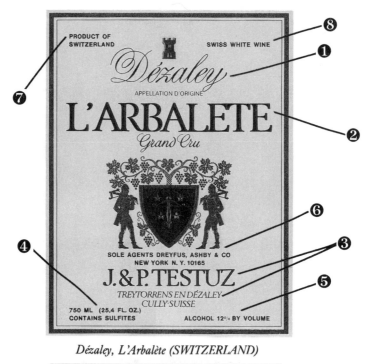

Dézaley, L'Arbalète (SWITZERLAND)

Fendant de Sion, Les Murettes (SWITZERLAND)

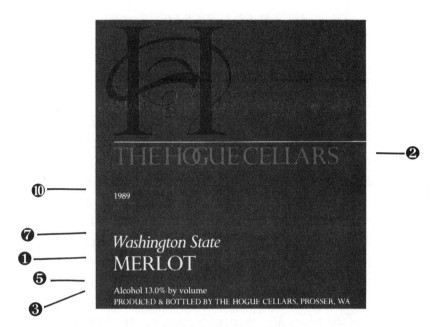

Merlot, Hogue Cellars (USA)

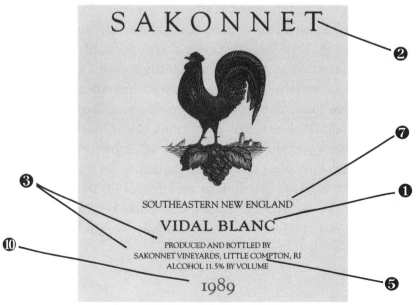

Vidal Blanc, Sakonnet (USA)

We deal with all of this every time we go grocery shopping and usually never give it a second thought, so there is no reason why we should have any problem with buying wine—the process by which we make use of the information on food labels in the grocery store is the same that we use when buying wine in a wine shop. We generally know what kind of food or wine we want, and the label is there as a guide to tell us if we're looking at the right type of item. (In the grocery store, it may be creamed corn; in the wine shop, Red Bordeaux.) Next we look to see who the producer is; if we don't recognize the name of the producer we may move on to another brand of corn or another maker of Red Bordeaux. We might then check the expiration date on the corn, or the vintage of the wine. And then, of course, we check the price on both the corn and the wine—most of us don't wait until the end to do this; some people, on the other hand, don't bother checking the price at all.

What about all the details about shipper, alcoholic content, and the rest? Well, just as we don't necessarily read all of the information that the law specifies must be on the creamed corn label (nutritional content, ingredients, etc.), so we don't necessarily have to pore over every item on the wine label. Of course, that information can be most helpful in making a complete and informed choice, but unless you are particularly diet- or nutrition-conscious (in the case of corn), or more specific in your preferences (in the case of wine) this is not strictly necessary. A simple reading of the main points of information can be sufficient to guide you in making a satisfactory choice of a wine.

12

Vintage,
and What
It Means

We now come to a topic thought by many to be one of the key criteria for judging a wine's quality: vintage. Yet, according to the list of label information in the previous chapter, it does not have to appear on the bottle.

The word "vintage" has several meanings in French, which can be a source of some confusion when it is left untranslated in books and articles about wine. To keep things uncomplicated here, we'll be using the word in just one sense: a wine's vintage is the year in which the grapes used to make that wine were picked. Thus, a wine with a vintage date of 1985 is made from grapes that were picked in that year. Simple, right? But the year 1985 on a label not only tells you that all the grapes used to make that wine were harvested in that year, but also much more—not just about the wine, but about the grapes themselves.

As mentioned in Chapter 7, the riper the grapes, the better the wine. The grapes' ripeness (and the size of the harvest) depends on the grapevine receiving the right amounts of warmth, rainfall, and sunshine at just the right time in its growing cycle. Everything must come together in the right proportions to achieve grapes (and wine) of maximum quality. Too much rain can be as detrimental as too little, and if the rainfall comes all at once during harvest time instead of evenly distributed throughout the spring and summer the results can be disastrous. (Just imagine if *you* had to go thirsty for six months at a time, and then all the water that had been denied you was delivered in one 300-gallon tank to be drunk in two or three days.)

Now, obviously, each year's weather pattern is different —that's what makes Ground Hog's Day so exciting—and in some years the weather will be more cooperative for the growing of good, ripe grapes than in others. In years that are too cold or too hot, too rainy or too dry, or just not sunny enough, winemakers have a number of options in both the vineyard and the winery to salvage what might otherwise be a lost harvest. These include: giving the grapes a greater or lesser amount of time on the vine before harvesting, throwing away a greater or lesser quantity of unripe grapes before crushing them, or either prolonging or shortening the fermentation time for the pressed juice in order to extract more or less tannin, color, and other substances into the wine. These decisions are never made for their own sake but to compensate for some imbalance in the weather during the growing year.

Each winemaker's solution will be different because each is working with grapes that have been affected by the weather in different ways. If Pierre's grapes are planted toward the top of a hill, they will be less affected by a heavy downpour than Jacques' grapes planted toward the bottom, whose roots are drowning in the run-off water from above. Or consider Henri's vines, which are planted on the southern face of a hill and receive direct sunshine throughout the day, while Jean's vines receive less light because they are located on the west-facing side of the hill and only get the rays of the afternoon sun; in a year of abundant sunshine, both Henri and Jean may harvest ripe grapes, but in a cloudier year Jean will have to struggle a little more to compensate.

So it is to the weather that we must look for the factor that defines the varying quality of a wine from one year to the next. After all, the ground that the grapevines are planted in does not change—if the side of a hill faced south in 1987, chances are very good that it continued to do so in 1988; if a grapevine was of a particular variety in 1987 (say, chardonnay or cabernet sauvignon, for instance), it most likely stayed that way in 1988; and, barring a change in ownership, if Pierre made the wine in 1987, he also made the wine in 1988. The land, the grapes, and the winemaker do not change from year to year; if a wine's style and quality depended on these factors alone, they would be consistent every year. The big variable in winemaking is the weather; no two years *ever* have the same weather, which is why there is a difference in a wine from one year to another and why the vintage on the label is so important.

But, as mentioned above, some wines do not have a vintage year on the label. Does this mean that these wines were made from grapes that were not harvested? Hardly; rather, these wines are made by blending the juice from grapes that were harvested in more than one single year. For some winemakers, being able to offer a product that is consistent year in and year out is more important than trying to create a magnificent wine one year and running the certain risk of being unable to duplicate it the next. And so, these winemakers will keep reserves of pressed grape juice or fermented wine from previous harvests; some may be from very ripe grapes, some from not so ripe ones. The winemaker blends the juice or wine from each new harvest with that of previous years to balance whatever faults or deficiencies may have resulted from variations in that year's weather. In this way, if the grapes in 1985 did not ripen as well as the winemaker would have liked, the juice from those grapes will be blended with that of 1982, which produced much riper grapes. Or if 1987 was a magnificent year with superb grapes capable of making a wonderful wine, the juice from that year will be blended with reserves from the weaker 1985 to create a more dilute, more mediocre, but more consistent wine based on that winemaker's style.

All of this is perfectly legal, and in theory it is conceivably possible to create a nonvintage wine that is better than one with a vintage on its label; a conscientious winemaker carefully working with juice from good-quality grapes can produce a better wine than an indifferent winemaker who uses mediocre grapes and simply slaps a label with a year onto the bottle. In general, however, wines without vintage years on the label may never be disappointingly poor, but they will never be breathtakingly excellent, either.

Having a vintage year printed on a label is all well and good, but how do we know whether it represents a growing season of good weather or bad? This is where vintage charts come in.

If you drink wine with any frequency, sooner or later you will come into contact with, or feel the need to consult, a vintage chart. This is a printed guide whose purpose is to give you a rating on the quality of the wine from a particular region in a given year. To say that sooner or later you will come across a vintage chart is an understatement—before you've uncorked (or unscrewed) your final bottle of wine in this life, you will have encountered dozens, scores, perhaps hundreds of these things as tables in the appendices of wine books (like this one), as handy pocket cards from retail shops, as brochures from wine importers and distributors, and in various other forms.

Vintage charts are a little like multiplication tables in their appearance, but unfortunately they are not quite as definitive. 2 × 2 may always equal 4, but just because a vintage chart may rate 1985 Red Bordeaux as outstanding doesn't mean that the 1985 Château Whatever you plan on having with dinner tonight is going to be the greatest thing since the automatic pencil sharpener.

A vintage chart is an indication of an individual's interpretation of the various factors that may have formed the general impression of the numerous types of wine from a given region in a given year. If this sounds a little nebulous, well, it is, and although the rating on the chart may appear to have the comforting appearance of solid fact, it doesn't.

The chart works like this: as we have seen, the weather directly affects the quality of the grapes grown during a given year, and by extension, the wine made from those grapes. The more closely the weather in a given year approximates the ideals of temperature, rainfall, hours of sunshine, and the like, the higher the esteem in which the wines from that year will be held. Thus, on a scale of 100, a year that is rated 90 will have had a better distribution and amount of rainfall, sunshine, and so on, than a year rated 85. Not every region in a country, let alone every country, however, will have the same weather; thus, the chart will not have just one rating for the year, but will be broken down with a rating for each region. This should take care of any differences between wines, right? Wrong. Unfortunately (or, perhaps, fortunately for the sake of variety), there are other factors that must be taken into account—remember Henri's southern-exposure vineyard and Jean's westerly-facing grapes? Some winemakers can make a good wine in a poor year (and vice versa); this is one reason why a vintage chart can only be a general guide and not holy writ.

Another reason is that although we are dealing with physical reality (a particular region's weather in 1988 was simply *not* as good as the weather in 1987), the interpretation of how well the winemakers were able to cope is entirely subjective, and as a result, so is the vintage chart. It can be confusing to see how one chart will rate a year more or less highly than another chart does, but it is important to remember that these charts are made by individuals, or groups of individuals, and as such are the products of personal preferences. There is no law stating who can make a vintage chart (indeed, you can sit down now and create your own if you wished), so discrepancies and variations are bound to exist among them. The best approach to using vintage charts is to remember that they can be useful as general guides, but are no more unanimous or absolute in their appraisal of a vintage than are Siskel and Ebert in judging a film.

One final word: as we've seen, vintage ratings are relative, and rather than refer to "good" and "poor" years, it might be more helpful to think of them as "good" and "not as good." Given today's understanding of winemaking and the modern technology available, "poor" vintages that produce absolutely undrinkable wine are largely a thing of the past; even in a year in which weather conditions are less than perfect, a good, satisfying (albeit not great) wine can still be made.

Such a wine will not necessarily be bad—it will merely be a shadow of what it can be in years of better weather. Its basic character would be the same, but compared to a wine from a "good" vintage, this one would be less intense in color, less aromatic in aroma, less rich in taste, and less capable of long aging. (There is a silver lining: because the wine is less complex it needs less time to pull itself together, so instead of needing 20 years to reach its peak, the wine may be ready to drink in four or five.)

This diminished quality is almost always offset by a diminished price as the winemaker must sell the wine for less than usual to compensate for that vintage's relatively poor showing. Depending on how slight the decrease in its quality and how great the decrease in its price, this can make a wine interesting enough to consider "trading up" and purchasing one that you've always heard about but that is ordinarily priced beyond your budget.

Imagine two Porsches. Both look alike and essentially drive the same, but instead of going from zero to 60 in four seconds, one of them does it in six and only gets a top speed of 90 instead of 130. Its performance is not up to standard Porsche specifications, and so the car is marked down in price—from $34,000 to $12,000. You've always heard about how good the car is, but at the full price it was never quite affordable. If for $12,000 you could have the same basic experience with just a relatively diminished performance, however, the $22,000 difference might make it worth sacrificing two seconds of acceleration and 40 mph at the top end of the scale. And even with its reduced specs, it can still give you a better ride than a $12,000 Volkswagen Jetta at its best.

Just as every car will not be equally interesting under such circumstances (a cheaper Yugo is still a Yugo), not every wine will be worthy of such bargain-hunting. Still, in a "not as good" vintage, the best winemakers are more likely to have the resources and expertise to make a wine that is better than one might expect in such difficult weather conditions. Its quality may be only a reflection of what it can be at its best, yet it can still be a good wine that is heads and shoulders above many others from better vintages.

Unfortunately, thanks to the knowledge and technology that have made "good" vintages so frequent, many wine drinkers have become spoiled and are no longer willing even to consider a good wine from a "not as good" vintage whose quality would have been considered more than satisfactory 20 or 30 years ago. This sort of snobbery causes a lot of people to overlook a lot of good wine.

Think of it this way: if you compare the results of the pole vault event from the 1968 and the 1988 Olympics, you'll see that in the latter games all of the losing jumpers still cleared the bar at heights greater than the gold medal winner of 20 years earlier. Thanks to technological developments in the pole's composition and superior technique by the athletes, even the average showings are still very impressive.

Similarly, the quality to be found in many wines from a "not as good" vintage would have been considered better than average 20 years ago. It is often said that the average level of quality for wine has never been higher than it is today, which means that much of the fear of getting stuck with an undrinkable bottle of wine is groundless. Therefore, while consulting a vintage chart can be helpful, you needn't feel that you must exclusively drink wines from only excellent years, or that you will poison yourself if you choose a wine in a restaurant or wine shop without having thoroughly memorized every vintage rating for the past 10 years. Trust yourself; chances are good that you'll do just fine.

CHEERS! ————————————

It can be extremely instructive to try two versions of the same wine from different years to get a clear idea of the importance of vintages. Unfortunately, when you go to the wine shop, most wines are available in only one vintage—namely, the most recent one. Stores and the distributors that service them will stock enough wine from a given vintage to last them until the new wine becomes available the following year.

In most good wine shops, however, it is usually possible to find certain wines in more than one vintage; these are the red wines from the Bordeaux region of France. The range of availability for this type of wine is due to the fact that producers in Bordeaux make relatively large quantities each year and the demand for their wines is consistently high. Therefore, stores and distributors will often have a supply of several vintages on hand. Unfortunately, most of the wines deemed sufficiently interesting to inspire a search for older vintages tend to be rather expensive. But so popular are the wines from this region, even some of the less renowned (and therefore less expensive) of them can be found in more than one vintage.

The labels below are meant to give you an idea of some moderately priced wine that you may find in multiple vintages; don't worry if you can't find the same wine or vintages

Margaux, Château de Clairefont 1987

shown here. If in doubt, ask a salesperson where you shop to suggest a wine they have available from more than one year.

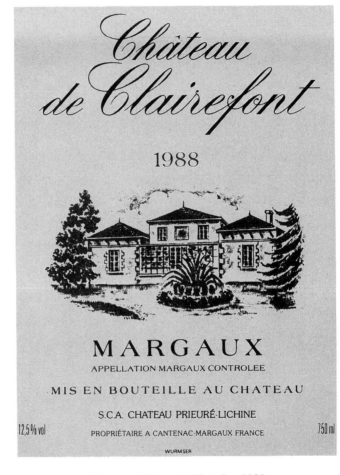

Margaux, Château de Clairefont 1988

13

How to Buy Wine in a Store

Unless you are blessed with a phenomenal popularity and are continually being treated to glasses and bottles of wine, the time will inevitably come when you must enter a store and make a selection yourself. Now while it's true that this involves making a choice that can mean the difference between satisfaction and disappointment when the wine is poured, the really important choice is not what to buy, but where to buy it. Once you've found the right place to shop, finding the right wine becomes as simple as making any other kind of purchase.

Wine can be bought in various types of stores; depending on where you live, it may be available in supermarkets and grocery stores as well as in wine shops. But in the same way that many people believe that you can get better meat at a butcher's shop than at the meat counter of a supermarket, there are those who will swear that good wines can only be found at a wine shop. This is not necessarily true—good wines are available practically anywhere, and depending on what you are looking for, a grocery store can meet your needs just as well as a specialty wine shop. Be it supermarket or wine shop, however, the important question is: how good is the quality of the store? This will be your most significant clue to the quality of the wines they offer.

Buying a bottle or two in the same place where you get the other ingredients for a lunch or dinner can be the ideal way to purchase your wine, and the variety available in food shops can generally satisfy most of your daily needs. The selection in these stores will be mostly wines for current consumption—something you'll drink with lunch or dinner within a couple of weeks after buying it—although more ambitious food stores may carry some items that are capable of improving with age.

Judging the quality of the merchandise for sale in the wine aisle is no different than judging quality throughout the rest of the store. If the produce department tends to have a fairly basic selection of fruits and vegetables, chances are the wine selection will be fairly basic, too. If the range of brands available in the soap or cereal sections is limited to only a few major names, the wine selection will be similarly limited in scope. Some stores simply do not have the space to offer a sizable assortment of wines, and thus stick with a basic selection of popular choices. But unless you are searching for a specific wine or a particular vintage, you should have no problem finding something acceptable to go with your meal.

But then there are other telltale signs that are more serious in their significance. Check out the canned food aisles: if the cans are dusty, misarranged on the shelf, or even severely dented or bulging, this is an obvious sign that the store is not particularly concerned with the condition or quality of the merchandise they sell; there's no reason to believe that the wines have received any better consideration, so chances are good that you will get a spoiled or mediocre bottle in such a place.

Even basic $3.99 wines require a minimum amount of care as they await their eventual sale, and just as the conditions for displaying frozen foods are rather particular, so it is with wine. A store doesn't have to construct a whole temperature- and humidity-controlled room for its wines, but there are certain minimum considerations that should be observed. Uncomfortably high temperatures for even a day or two can spoil a wine, so if you see bottles or cases stacked near radiators or steam pipes you might wish to consider another store for your wine needs. Prolonged exposure to bright light—like the spotlights highlighting a special promotion—can cause deterioration of a wine's quality (that's why they put it in green and brown tinted bottles), but the fluorescent lights in the ceiling shouldn't have any noticeable effect on the wine. Don't be too critical if the bottles are standing up on the shelf instead of lying on their sides; most food stores don't want to bother installing special bins to keep horizontally stacked bottles from rolling off the shelf onto the floor. In any case, for the few months that a bottle may be left standing, it's unlikely that its cork will dry out and spoil the wine inside.

The best of all possible worlds is a store with a good-sized wine department that shows signs of care in its selection and upkeep. Supermarkets usually have a manager responsible for each of the different sections of the store; ask to see whoever is in charge of the wine aisle and try to get an impression of how interested that person is in the merchandise. The manager should be as familiar with the wines as the meat manager is with the contents of the refrigerated cases. Expect nothing less from the wine aisle than you would from any other department in the store.

Of course, if you wanted something more exotic than tomatoes or celery you would go to a greengrocer. Similarly, if you are looking for a particular type of wine from a specific producer in a certain vintage, your chances of finding it are better at a wine shop. But not every store that sells wine is necessarily a wine shop. A lot of places are better described as liquor stores—their main stock in trade is scotch, vodka, gin and other beverages made from grain instead of grapes; their wine selection generally consists of a couple of bottles on some shelves in the back. The owner and salespeople are not particularly interested in these bottles and only stock them because their license says they can. A wine shop has a more balanced distribution of shelf space, and it is here that you would go in search of that particular wine you liked at a restaurant or a friend's house. A good sign that a store is fairly serious about their selection is if some wines are available in more than one vintage; this generally shows that the store is concerned with the depth of their selection as well as its breadth.

A wine shop should not be judged for quality on the size of its inventory; because there is such a wide assortment of wine available in the world, no store can be expected to carry everything. Some stores will therefore specialize in wines from a particular area, such as Spain or Italy, while carrying a representative selection of the other wines of the world.

The abundant choice available in most wine shops can be a little intimidating, and will sometimes keep people from ever venturing inside. But one of the wonderful things about wine *is* that great variety. If you find something that you like you can always stay with it; there's nothing wrong with that. But if you enjoy the experience of discovering new pleasures, you will never run out of possibilities. In either case the question remains: unless there is something specific that you seek, how among the hundreds of bottles on display can you find a wine that you'll like?

For starters, keep in mind that the shop owner gains nothing by making it difficult for you to find a wine. It's simple retail logic: every type of shop is arranged according to some system, whether it is a hardware store with power tools to the front, nails and ball bearings toward the rear; women's apparel, with shoes and gloves to the left, skirts and blouses to the right; or bookstores, where the novels are in aisle 3 and the cookbooks in aisle 8. A wine shop is no different, and even though all those bottles may seem alike, a closer look at the layout of the store will show that they are arranged in some sort of order, usually by place of origin. The best way to get a feel for the manner in which the inventory has been organized is to simply browse. It sounds ridiculously simple, but relatively few people ever do it. The only time some folks ever enter a wine shop is on the way to a party or dinner, dashing in and simply picking up the first bottle in the appropriate price range with a nice label. Try this instead: stop in a wine shop on the way home from work and spend five or 10 minutes just looking at the bottles. Read the labels; see what neighboring bottles have in common; try and understand the rhyme and reason behind the way the wines are arranged. Don't worry about the prices for now; you don't have to buy anything (although it wouldn't be a bad opportunity to get something for that evening's dinner). After a few visits a pattern will emerge and you'll begin to feel more at home among all those bottles.

In addition, a good wine shop has a resource at your disposal that sets it apart from the supermarkets and liquor stores, a resource dedicated to helping you find your way among all the bottles on display and zero in on the wine for you. It is called a wine salesperson. At its best, this resource can be the key to answering every question you may ever have about all those many bottles that surround you. At its worst, you have little more than a vending machine on two feet. As with every resource, its effectiveness depends on communicating with it as best you can—the more specific you are, the more satisfied you are likely to be with the results.

It's like using the library: if you ask the librarian for something on sports, you may simply be directed to the encyclopedia. But if you are more specific and indicate that you want information on the team batting averages for the 1959 Dodgers, you'll get the *Baseball Almanac*, which is what you wanted all along, even if you didn't know to ask for it. The salesperson in the wine shop is like that librarian in the library; the more specific you can be about what you want, the more helpful the salesperson can be. "I want a white wine" is pretty general, and with such a request you can end up with a Hungarian dessert wine that costs $50 a bottle, when all you wanted was a little something to have with the tuna casserole for dinner.

Unless you know specifically what type of wine you are seeking ("Do you have a bottle of Château Whatever, 1987?"), it's best not to *say* what you want but rather *explain* what you need, as specifically as possible: "I'm having tuna casserole for dinner tonight; do you have a fairly simple white wine, perhaps from California or France, for about $6 or $7?"

The last part is important—to help narrow down the possibilities available, be sure to tell the salesperson how much you want to spend, even if money is no object. Many people are needlessly sheepish about asking for a wine at the low end of the price scale. Most sales help in wine shops do not work on commission, so it is all the same to them if you spend $5 or $500 on a bottle of wine. A reputable merchant will take pains to see that there are good quality wines available at every price level, so you shouldn't worry about getting stuck with a bottle of vinegar if you spend less than $7.50 on your choice.

One of the benefits that a wine shop can offer is the personalized service of dealing with a salesperson, and if you buy wine with any frequency you should make it a point to seek out the same salesperson each time, preferably one who has shown a particular knowledge of wines and a willingness to share it with you. Establish a commercial relationship;

make that salesperson *your* salesperson, and gradually your preferences and tastes will become known in the shop, thereby streamlining the process of finding a suitable wine each time you stop by.

Some wine shops print a catalog of their offerings, and it is a good idea to get on their mailing list and have a copy sent to you. This offers several advantages. It gives you the opportunity to browse at your leisure and narrow your choices in advance of entering the store, saving you and your salesperson a lot of time later. Try to receive catalogs from more than one shop, and then compare prices to find the best values available. (Be sure that your comparisons are for wines of the same type, from the same producer, in the same vintage; you wouldn't expect the price of last year's Subaru to bear any relation to the price of this year's Audi, would you?)

There is one feature common to many wine shops that is especially interesting: the discount bin. This is usually an old wine barrel or wooden crate filled with an assortment of bottles that have been marked down in price. Wines will find their way here in one of two ways. Perhaps the shop has only a few bottles left of a particular wine, a quantity so small that it is no longer practical to continue advertising it in the catalog or have it taking up precious shelf space. Thus, the discount bin acts as a sort of in-store advertisement to promote a quicker sale. Or maybe the wine in the bin is on its last legs and has already passed its peak of drinkability—it may still be a pleasant enough wine, but the owner feels unjustified in charging the regular price for it. The trick is in knowing whether the wine in question is just beginning its decline or is well on the way to decrepitude. It's also largely a matter of personal taste—some people prefer the character of an older wine, and when conventional opinion states that a given vintage may have passed its peak, these people are just finding it drinkable.

Sometimes there are true bargains to be found in the discount bin, but there are also risks, too. The best way to deal with the bin is to spend no more on a wine than you feel you won't regret if it turns out to be a disappointment. But rest assured: even if you're never tempted by anything in the discount bin, there'll still be enough wine on the shelves to keep you happily occupied.

14

Storing Wine

As with any type of food, be it fresh fish or olive oil, wine must be stored properly to keep it from going bad. Happily, this is not difficult; for the most part it's a matter of simple common sense. But because of a singular characteristic unique to wine, the question of storage takes on an added dimension.

Unlike all other foods, which can only spoil or, at best, remain unchanged, wine has the capacity to improve with time. The function of storing wine, therefore, is not just to keep it handy until you decide to open and serve it, but to develop its latent quality that reflects the effort and expense of the winemakers in growing the grapes and turning them into wine.

The exact conditions under which wine will successfully mature in the bottle are poorly understood because no one is certain exactly how or why this change occurs. This has not prevented the development of an entire canon of quite specific rules dictating how cool, how humid, how quiet, and how long a wine must be stored to bring about its metamorphosis. Unfortunately, much of this information is little better than folklore, so there's no sense in becoming confused or intimidated by it all. And you needn't worry that your wine can never mature—or worse, will turn to vinegar—if you do not have a full-fledged wine cellar at your disposal.

Just as the glass bottle and cork stopper comprise the "traditional ideal" for packaging wine, the cellar is considered the "traditional ideal" for its storage. The trouble with tradition in these nontraditional times is that few of us have access to a cool, dark cellar where wine can rest undisturbed. But this should not deter anyone from buying the odd bottle or two; although wine can be somewhat particular as to the surroundings it prefers, it is not as delicate as is popularly believed. Wine can mature in locations less cool and isolated than the depths of a cellar, and can tolerate quite a lot before it slides over the edge into spoilage.

If a cool, dark cellar is not available, a (relatively) cool, dark closet can work, too. You can also keep your bottles under the bed or sofa, in a spare dresser drawer, or in a dark corner under the steps. What is important is that the chosen location should be stable in temperature and shielded from continuous exposure to light.

The average wine cellar is around 55°F, but you can safely keep wines at temperatures 10 degrees higher, or more. Higher temperatures will simply accelerate a wine's aging, making it ready to drink sooner. While this won't necessarily spoil it, remember that the longer a wine takes to reach maturity, the more satisfying it will eventually be.

It's not so much the temperature that's important, but its fluctuation. Changes in temperature can cause the bottle's contents to expand and contract, putting stress on the cork's air-tight seal. This increases the danger of air getting into the bottle and spoiling the wine. Telltale signs of this are rivulets of dried wine coming from under the foil capsule and staining the bottle and label (this is easier to see with reds than with whites), or a bulge under the capsule indicating a cork that has been pushed out above the lip of the bottle.

Light, particularly sunlight, can cause deterioration in a wine, and so is best avoided, too. If you purchase wine by the case, simply leave the bottles in the box it comes in and you've solved that problem.

You can see that since there are only two major factors that can have an adverse effect on wine, your options are quite open in choosing a place to store it. Indeed, it's easier to list the locations that would be unsuitable for the purpose: stay away from any place in the vicinity of steam pipes or heating ducts; try to avoid the kitchen, and especially those open wine racks made to fit above the cabinets near the ceiling—not only will the wine be exposed to almost constant light, but it will also be fully exposed to the heat rising up from the stove whenever you cook; and don't use the garage if it tends to get very cold in the winter and hot in the summer.

Now, not every wine is made with the idea that it will improve with time; most wines, in fact, are made to be enjoyed soon after purchase—these are our "current consumption" wines, the ones you pick up on the way home to have with dinner that evening. Most white wines and inexpensive to moderately priced reds are in this category. These wines require no special handling, since a couple of days perched on top of the refrigerator will not seriously affect them.

How can you tell if the wine you're interested in buying falls in the current consumption category or is a candidate for long-term aging? Just ask your wine salesperson; if the wine requires aging, you'll also find out when it might be ready for drinking.

If you should find yourself in the position of amassing more bottles than you can comfortably manage at home, or if you decide to buy your wines by the case and don't care to have dozens of bottles continually underfoot, storage facilities exist that will hold your wine in climate-controlled surroundings. Some good wine shops make this service available to their customers for a modest fee; inquire if yours can do this for you or if they could recommend a company that can. (Keep in mind that this is the sort of care that you would only lavish on wines requiring aging, since it's hard to justify such expenditure on current consumption wines.)

One last question on the subject of keeping wine from going bad: what should you do with an open bottle that is only partially consumed? The main point here is that a half-full bottle will have a lot more air in contact with the wine than one that is unopened. As we have seen, air in small doses can gradually age a wine, and in large doses (as with a half-full bottle) will quickly spoil it. So what to do with that partially full bottle? Well, regardless of whether the leftover wine is red or white, simply push the cork back in the bottle and put it in the refrigerator. The wine in the recorked bottle will still begin losing quality fairly rapidly, and obviously it will not taste exactly the same as when it was first opened, but it will remain reasonably drinkable for the next 3 to 5 days (if the bottle were not recorked at all the wine would be lucky to last 24 hours); after that, you can use the bottle's contents in a salad dressing.

There are other solutions to the problem of saving leftover wine. One of the best is simply to purchase half-bottles. Not everything comes in this size (375 ml), but depending on where you shop, a pretty good selection may be available. Another solution makes use of the previous one: clean and save several empty 375s, and when you have wine from a regular-size bottle left at the end of a meal simply transfer it to the smaller container and recork. Now you have a full bottle once again (or close to it), with much less air in contact with the wine than would be the case were it left in the full-sized 750 ml bottle. A full, recorked half-bottle will not last as long as one that has never been opened, but it will significantly outlast the partially filled 750.

15

Serving Wine

Serving wine at home should simply be a matter of opening a bottle and pouring it into the glass, and in truth there is really not much more to it than that. (Restaurant wine service is another story, and we'll look at that in the next chapter.) But whether it is for reasons of convenience, tradition, or personal preference, every food has certain "fine points" that come into question when serving. (For instance, is turkey served with the stuffing in the bird or on the side? Should spaghetti be eaten with a fork and spoon or just a fork? Are soft pretzels best when eaten with or without mustard?) Wine service has its fine points too, and they are often similarly inconsequential to the enjoyment of the wine itself.

Assuming that you have chosen a wine to drink, the first thing that must be done is to open the bottle. Unless your wine is in a screw-top container or a bag-in-a-box, you'll have to pull a cork from the bottle, and there are numerous tools for doing this. Most fall into the "gadget" category, like the pump that injects air through a needle to force the cork out of the bottle. (This has been known to explode bottles if there is a flaw in the glass.) Another popular device is a two-pronged utensil that has the ability to extract a cork without puncturing it. (This has been known to chip the glass inside the bottle's neck, requiring the wine to be strained through cheesecloth—or if you're drinking directly from the bottle, through your teeth.) But since this book is intended as a guide to getting the wine into your glass with the least amount of fuss and not as an encyclopedia of bottle openers, we'll simply focus on the basic corkscrew.

Corkscrews are available in a tremendous variety of styles, but regardless of their design, the one feature common to them all, by definition, is a "screw" that gets twisted into the cork. There are two types of screw, one good and one to be avoided. What you want to look for is this: a screw made of thick, sturdy wire twisted into a spiral and tapering down to a point. The vital requirement is that the spiral be an open one—that is, you should be able to stick a hairpin right through the center of it. The bad style of screw is actually a type of gimlet—a solid shaft, like an awl, with a wedge spiraling around it. What makes the design so poor for its purpose is that instead of making just a small hole in the cork, this bores into the stopper and splits it open, often leaving half of it in the bottle. To make matters worse, you then have to spend time fishing out pieces of cork from your wine.

The first step in opening the bottle is to remove the capsule, whose purpose is to protect the cork and keep it clean. If it is made of plastic, look for the pull-tab that makes it simple to remove; if there is no tab, you may elect to open another bottle of wine, since those thick plastic capsules are next to impossible to remove otherwise. If the capsule is made of foil, you can either trim away only the top to expose the cork or remove it entirely—it makes no difference whatsoever to the taste of the wine. (If you do decide to trim away only the top, be sure to cut the capsule below the thick ring on the neck called the "bead"; this is because the capsule is still often made traditionally, from lead foil. Now, should the wine come into contact with the lead, it won't make you keel over right there at the table; but it is best to be prudent, and there is less chance of the wine touching the capsule if it is cut well away from the opening of the bottle.)

Next, insert the point of the screw into the cork, pressing gently to get the hole started, and simply twist it in. (In general, corkscrews are designed to be turned clockwise, but this is by no means universal; in any event, it will soon become apparent if you're turning in the wrong direction.) Once the screw is seated in the cork there's no need to continue pressing down while twisting, as this will only risk pushing the stopper into the bottle.

The method for actually extracting the cork will vary significantly depending on the type of corkscrew you have. Some are self-extracting: that is, as you continue to turn the screw, the cork is automatically pulled up from the bottle. (A device called the Screwpull is perhaps the best of these—in fact, the Screwpull is probably the best tool for pulling corks, period, and I heartily recommend investing in one—they cost under $20, and are well worth it; see page 136.) Other

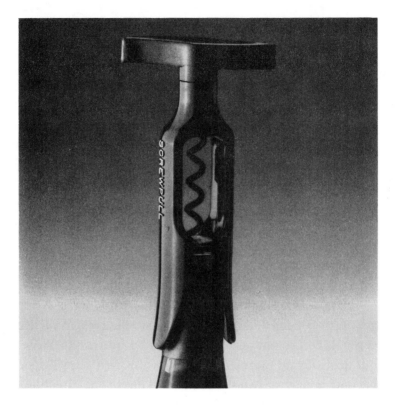

corkscrews may have a lever that hooks onto the rim of the bottle so you can pivot the cork out (this is the type that is commonly used by waiters and is quite reliable). Still others require you to use simple muscle-power to pull the cork from the bottle. If you have this type of corkscrew, just twist it until the screw is fully embedded in the cork. Then put the bottle on the floor between your feet, with the base squarely on the ground. (You can put the bottle between your legs, but you will risk spilling wine on your clothes when the bottle jerks as the cork is pulled.) Use one hand to hold the bottle firmly in place by pressing down on the neck, and use the other hand to pull up with equal force to remove the cork. Be careful: if the base is not squarely on the ground, you run the risk of slamming the bottle against the floor and breaking it once the cork comes free. Also, when pulling the cork, be sure that the force comes *from your arm and not your back*, otherwise you could end up walking hunched over for a long time. If all of this makes opening a bottle of wine seem to be more trouble than it's worth, throw that type of corkscrew away, get a Screwpull, and open your wine standing upright like a normal, self-respecting *Homo sapiens*.

Finally, use a damp cloth to wipe the lip of the bottle clean of anything (mold, capsule residue, etc.) that may have collected there.

We've already discussed the appropriate type of wine glass in Chapter 6, but to repeat: feel free to use whatever type of glasses you have. There's no need to invest in a whole set of stemware just to enjoy a little wine with dinner.

All that remains is to pour the wine, and here is the only tricky part of the entire operation: be careful to get it in the glass and not on the table, yourself, or anybody else; this is especially important when pouring red wine. (Household hint: if you should happen to spill some red wine, you can wash it out right away with white wine—the proteins that set the stain so firmly are the same in both types of wine, so you are in effect replacing the red wine proteins with those from the white, which don't stain.)

And that's really all there is to serving and enjoying wine.

Except for those questions that are usually matters of personal taste. To wit:

Temperature. The basic guideline is that white wines should be served chilled, red wines at room temperature. But too often white wines end up being served so chilled that you can't taste anything in the glass—the cold simply numbs the tastebuds. As for red wines, "room temperature" is really a tad too warm, with the result that the tannins become too pronounced and the wine seems harsh.

So, if white wines are generally served too cold and red wines are served too warm, what should you do? The best advice comes from wine importer Peter Sichel, who recommends the following: allow the white wine to chill for several hours in the refrigerator (not the freezer) until fifteen minutes before serving, at which time it should be taken from the fridge to remove some of the chill; for red wines, put the bottle *in* the refrigerator fifteen minutes before serving to bring its temperature down to a more pleasant level for drinking. (Of course, there is no law that forbids drinking a red wine chilled, and for some wines that are light in tannins this can be quite refreshing, especially in summer.)

Breathing. There are two main reasons for letting a wine "breathe." Occasionally a wine may develop certain off-odors that do not indicate anything fundamentally wrong with it, but are simply a normal by-product of bottle aging. These gases will dissipate after the cork is pulled, and breathing can help speed this process along.

A second reason for letting a wine breathe is to help release its aroma. By facilitating the wine's interaction with the air, its aromatic molecules become more readily detected by the nose. (A wine in which the aroma stays trapped in the liquid is said to be "closed"; when the aroma becomes more noticeable, the wine is said to have "opened up.")

Letting a wine breathe is by no means mandatory, and you may go through your entire wine-drinking life without ever feeling the need to do this. But should you come across a wine that you think would benefit from such treatment, it can be done in several different ways.

The most widely known method is to simply uncork the bottle a certain time in advance of pouring the wine. In principle, this brings air into contact with the wine, but the amount of surface area that is exposed is so small—only about the diameter of a dime—that to achieve any noticeable result would practically require opening the wine the night before. A more effective method is to open the wine in advance and pour it into the wine glasses. This exposes much more surface area to the air, and consequently helps the wine open up in less time. But if you prefer to open and serve the wine in front of your guests, you can first pour the wine into a carafe or some other suitable container and then into the wine glasses, thus incorporating air into the wine as it is transferred from one receptacle to another. But the following method is perhaps the easiest: open the wine and serve everyone; then each person can simply swirl the wine in their glass to dissipate any off-odor that may be present as well as incorporate air into the wine to release its aroma.

Decanting. This is occasionally done to remove the solid particles that can form in older red wines. These particles are known as "sediment" or a "deposit." Sediment generally won't appear in wines younger than eight years old, and often doesn't turn up until much later than that. (It never occurs in white wines.) Sediment is a natural part of the aging process and is not harmful to the wine or to you. But even though it is a natural part of wine, it will interfere with your enjoyment of it by introducing solid matter into what should be a purely liquid experience; you wouldn't care to have sediment in your glass any more than you'd appreciate coffee grounds in your cup. The remedy is to carefully pour the wine off into another container as described in the previous paragraph on letting a wine breathe, making sure that only the clear wine is transferred and the deposit remains behind in the bottle.

Unless the sight of a wine bottle on the table is particularly disturbing, you need never decant a white wine or a young red one. Decanting such wines can be little more than an ostentatious bit of snobbery that does nothing for the wine and only serves to make extra work by producing one more thing that must be washed at the end of the meal.

16

How to Buy Wine in a Restaurant

Just as we don't eat all of our meals at home, neither will we be drinking all of our wine there. This is where restaurants come in: they are in the business of selling both food *and* drink, and it is important to remember that food is only half of the equation when it comes to dining out.

It used to be that unless you went to a fancy, "white tablecloth" establishment or a neighborhood Italian restaurant, your choice of a beverage was usually limited to either soda or beer. But today, more and more places offer not only a house red and house white by the glass, but a selection of other wines as well. Although the variety available in restaurants is greater than ever before, deciding what to have with your meal should be a simple matter, requiring none of the elaborate strategies or games of one-upmanship with the wine waiter that are generally believed to be essential to the process. Indeed, ordering a wine should really be no more complex than ordering the food to eat with it.

Every restaurant serving more than a single selection will have a wine list, just as any restaurant serving more than one dish will have a menu. It may be a separate listing, it may be printed on the back of the menu, or it may be written on a chalkboard on the wall, but it will be available in some form. Ironically enough, although the wine list is intended to make selecting a wine easier, people can feel so uncomfortable about it that it often acts as a primary obstacle to that end.

For many, wine lists are as mysterious as the Egyptian Book of the Dead, full of unknown names whose significance is hard to remember and that are even harder to pronounce. About the only things that are readily understandable in it are the prices, and what is understandable about them is that they are generally too high.

Basically, the wine list is not unlike the program at a baseball game—just as you can't tell the players without a scorecard, you can't tell the wines without the wine list. The baseball program gives us all the information we need to know about who is playing, and what we can expect of each player by telling us their positions. The wine list is intended to tell us similarly important information. Let's look at it in detail.

First of all, just as the program at a ball game tells us the connection that a group of players share—their team—the wine list should tell us the wines' connection by grouping them together by color and place of origin: White Burgundies, Red Bordeaux, and so on. Next we must know the name of the wine just as we must know the names of the players. But the name of the ballplayer or the wine alone is not enough—occasionally there may be two players on a team with the same name. For example, the Oakland Athletics have had two Hendersons on the team playing neighboring positions in the outfield; but one wears number 24, the other number 42. With wines it is not unheard of for two different ones to have the same name. Such is the case with two wines named Château Latour: both are French, but one is a decent little white wine from a place called Entre-Deux-Mers, and the other is a great red wine from a town called Pauillac. To know which one is being offered, the wine list must indicate where the wine comes from, or who made it. Like a ballplayer's number, the place of origin or the winemaker's name is the detail that prevents any confusion about a wine's identity, and so is an essential part of the wine list.

The wine list should also include the wine's vintage, which gives you a clue as to the relative quality of the bottle in question, just as a player's batting average gives you an idea of how satisfying his performance is likely to be when he steps up to the plate.

To make the analogy complete, the baseball program should include the players' salaries just as the wine list gives the wines' prices, but you can carry analogies only so far. Only after you have been given all of this information can you begin to consider whether the price asked for a wine is worth paying.

(Some wine lists will include another detail for each

entry: a bin number. This is a sort of catalog number to help the server locate the wine in the cellar quickly and accurately. Should you be unsure how to pronounce the name of a particular wine, feel free to refer to it by its bin number: "I'd like a bottle of number 127, please.")

As with just about everything else in the world, when it comes to wine lists there are good ones and there are bad ones. A bad list is one that is incomplete in its information or so poorly designed that it can be more of a hindrance than an aid. This is why you shouldn't shy away from the wine list, but rather seek it out whenever you can, even if you don't order anything from it. After a while, you'll begin to recognize the good lists and even be able to understand some of what the bad ones are trying to tell you. Appendix B provides an example of a bad wine list, and an example of a good list with the same selection of wines written in a more easily understandable fashion.

Even with a well-designed list you may feel that you don't have enough experience to comfortably decide on which wine to order. Should this be the case, you needn't forgo having a wine with your meal. This is where the wine waiter comes in.

A lot of people feel intimidated by wine waiters. For starters, in fancy restaurants they are called *sommeliers*, which can be tricky to pronounce, and they know all about something of which you know nothing (or at least not as much as you'd like). But look at it this way: everybody knows more about something than someone else, and if you're, say, an auto mechanic and a wine waiter brings a car into your shop for repairs, you don't expect that person to know as much as you do about cars, do you? Good wine waiters understand that more important than an encyclopedic knowledge of wines is the ability to help you feel comfortable in choosing one to have with your meal. Thus, they will be generous with their knowledge and be happy to answer your questions in order to help you select a satisfying wine at a price you can afford.

Keep in mind that not all restaurants will have a wine waiter, someone whose sole job is to be familiar with every selection on the wine list and to share that familiarity with you, should you require help in making a choice. Most restaurants today will leave the wines to the server who handles the food order. Unfortunately, not all servers will have an understanding of wine, and may know even less than you about the subject. These are the people who are most likely to fulfill your fears of asking a dumb question about the wine list, since for them *any* question is dumb. If you should encounter a server who treats your questions as an insult to common sense, understand that you are merely running into someone's inferiority complex, and just fall back on one of two options—simply order a glass of the house wine or follow your own instincts, which can't be any worse than those of the "resident expert" (your server).

So, now that you know that there's no reason to be uneasy with the wine list and that the wine waiter is there to help and not to terrorize you, how to begin? Well, if you haven't ordered much wine in restaurants and are unsure of how to get your bearings, start off by asking if they have a house wine. Almost every place offers a red and white wine by the glass and your server will be happy to tell you what they are; as part of their spiel, they'll even identify which is the red and which is the white so if you don't remember what kind Chardonnay is, you won't have to wonder what color will be in your glass when it comes to the table.

Having ordered a glass of the house wine, ask to see the wine list (if it's not already on the table or printed on the back of the menu). You may want to try a bottle of something if there are enough wine drinkers at the table and you all feel so inclined. But even if you don't want a bottle of wine, still take the time to look at the list; remember, if you're not familiar with a wine list it will help you get used to the way they are laid out, the different kinds of wine available, and their prices. When the server returns for your wine order you can simply say that you prefer to stay with the house wine for now.

When a wine has been ordered, it will be brought to the table and presented to whomever made the choice. This is more than a simple courtesy, but rather a chance to make sure that it is indeed the same wine that was requested. It doesn't often happen but there may be a discrepancy, so it is wise to look at the following three things: *the name of the wine*—accidents do happen, and the server may simply have pulled a bottle from the wrong bin; *the name of the producer*—the type of wine may be the same as the one on the wine list (Beaujolais, Chablis, Chianti, etc.), but the producer may be different from the one listed, which as we have seen can make all the difference in the quality of the wine; *the vintage*—this is the detail on the bottle that is most likely to differ from what is printed in the wine list. Nothing lasts forever, and when a restaurant has run out of its supply of

1987s, they'll simply switch over to the available 1988s, often without updating their wine lists or even telling the servers. Now if 1988 was a better year than 1987 and you know this for a fact, then you might wish to say nothing. But if you are unsure about this or are at all uncomfortable about the change, feel free to send the bottle back (just as you would if the server brought you salmon and you ordered sole), and make another choice from the wine list. And don't let the server tell you that "there's no difference"—reread Chapter 12 if you've any doubt about that.

Assuming that the wine presented is the wine that was ordered, the server will proceed to open the bottle. Part of the procedure is to present the cork, which is actually done for practical reasons, although they are not the ones that are usually thought of. We've all seen the movies where the suave, debonair connoisseur deftly picks up the cork and brings it to the nostrils, sniffing to detect—what? Well, next time you're having wine at home, pick up the cork and sniff it. What do you smell? Cork, which should come as no surprise. The theory goes that by smelling the cork you can tell whether it has gone bad and tainted the wine. Perhaps, but it would seem that the same result would be arrived at with somewhat more accuracy by smelling the wine itself. (If you should have any doubts about the condition of the cork, squeeze it between your thumb and forefinger, particularly the wet end that was in contact with the wine. If the cork crumbles this could be a sign that it may not have been completely effective in keeping air from getting into the bottle.) No, the cork is presented not to be smelled, but to be read. You see, it has not been unknown for a superior label to be pasted onto a bottle of inferior wine—and sold for a superior price, of course. To prevent this type of deception, winemakers brand their corks with the name of the producer and the vintage to protect the consumer and the wine's reputation. This sort of fraud is rare today but all the same, when the cork is presented and if there is information stamped on it, take a glance to make sure that it agrees with what is on the label. (It is also for this reason that the wine bottle is *always* opened in front of the customer at the table—nothing could be easier than to pour who-knows-what into a bottle and then show a label and cork representing a different wine of superior quality.)

The server will pour a bit of the wine into the glass for inspection. This is to give the person who ordered the wine an opportunity to detect any flaws that would prevent an enjoyment of it. This whole process should take only a few seconds; there will be time enough later for a fuller appreciation of the wine without monopolizing the server's time. There are many things that the wine can tell you, but if you are not all that familiar (or concerned) with the subtleties present, all you need do is look for any obvious flaws.

First, look at the wine's color. Unless you are having a very old wine, there should be no brown tones in either whites or reds; while this may be acceptable in an aged wine, this can indicate improper storage in a younger one.

Next, swirl the wine in the glass to help release the aroma. There will be many smells coming up at you, but there are only two that you need be concerned with at this moment—the smell of vinegar, which suggests that the wine has turned sour; and the smell of cork, which indicates that the wine has been affected by a bad stopper. (See Chapter 10 for details about this problem.) Cork is not a particularly unpleasant smell, and to someone who is unaware that it signals a problem it can be overlooked as just another component of the wine's aroma. But the wine that is so affected will not taste the way the winemaker intended it to, and it was on the basis of that taste that the wine's price was set. Therefore, you simply won't be getting your money's worth from a corked wine.

Finally, taste the wine. What you are looking for is confirmation of any suspicion that the look or the smell of the wine may have given you. Don't feel obligated to deliver a complete analysis of the wine or even to come up with anything particularly clever to say. Unless there is some problem with the wine, all you need do is turn to the server and say, "Thank you." That will be the signal for the wine to be poured into everyone's glasses.

Of course, if there is a problem with the wine this is the moment to make it known to the server (not after everyone has consumed three-quarters of the bottle). In general, you need not worry too much about getting a bottle that has to be returned, or of missing some flaw that someone else at the table will pick up on. Problem bottles occur much less frequently than most people think. In any event, there are basically two telltale signs, and you don't have to be an expert to notice them: the unmistakably brown color of an improperly handled wine, and the vinegary or corky smell of a wine gone bad after bottling. These are pretty incontestable faults, and the restaurant should have no problem in opening another bottle for you.

If you order a type of wine that you've had before, but this time from an unfamiliar winemaker or vintage and find that it does not suit your taste, this does not constitute grounds for returning it. The wine may not have the pronounced aroma that you expected, which may be characteristic of that particular winemaker's style, or it may just need a little time in the glass to "open up." As long as the wine is sound, the restaurant has fulfilled its responsibility in the matter. If you ordered a beer and found it "skunky" or stale the bartender would pour you another, but if you ordered a Coors and then found that you preferred the taste of the Budweiser you're used to, you couldn't reasonably expect to get a new beer. It's the same with wine.

If the whole question of ordering wine still makes you uneasy, there's another option available. Occasionally a new restaurant will be ready to open for business, but because of red tape they have not yet received their liquor license. Rather than lose business waiting for the paperwork to go through, they'll open without the license and serve only food, inviting you to bring your own wine which they'll open and serve with your meal. This deal is through once their license arrives, although there are some restaurants that will allow you to bring your own wine and will charge you a "corkage fee" of several dollars. And then there are those rare restaurants that will not bother with getting a liquor license and simply invite you to bring your own wine as standard policy. They feel that whatever profit might be lost by forgoing the standard restaurant markup for wines (generally 200 to 250 percent over the retail price) is made up by the increased number of customers who will be attracted by the prospect of drinking a good bottle of wine (their own) at a more reasonable price. Be on the lookout for these restaurants—not only will you save money by bringing your own bottle, but you know that you won't be sending the wine back.

17

Wine and Food

One of the major obstacles to an enjoyment of wine is the anxiety surrounding the question of which ones are best suited for which foods. Unfortunately, since wine is made to be consumed with food, this question (and its attendant anxiety) arises virtually every time we purchase a bottle. There would seem to be few who can escape its potential for sowing the seeds of doubt: people who never worry about what clothes to wear when going out in public or what music to put on the stereo when having company at home suddenly find themselves facing a life and death choice when it comes to deciding what to drink with dinner, even if they're only dining alone.

For reassurance, one can always fall back on all sorts of guidelines and rules of thumb like "red wine with red meats and white wine with white meats." But like trying to remember whether it's "feed a fever and starve a cold," or "starve a fever and feed a cold," these guidelines can often give rise to more contemplation than is reasonable for the uncomplicated enjoyment of a simple glass of wine.

How did things get this way? Well, like much that is arcane and obscure about what should be a simple and easily appreciated pleasure, the ideal marriages of wine and food were established by people with far too much time on their hands (and money at their disposal), giving them the luxury of constructing an entire system of harmonious and exclusive concordances of solid and liquid nourishment.

Although rules for wine and food pairings are written in numerous books, these rules are not written in stone; many combinations that were once accepted as absolute expressions of immutable good taste are today thought to be bizarre at best, indigestible at worst (which naturally leads to speculation about the future verdict on what is currently taken as gastronomic holy writ).

Now, this is not to say that these combinations may not be pleasing or successful, only that they are not exclusive or infallible. When it comes to matching food and wine, we are not speaking of rules by which civilization stands or falls, but of something on a more modest and transitory scale, like fashion.

Once again, as with virtually every aspect of winemaking and wine drinking, we are dealing with questions of individual taste. It's all a matter of *opinion* as to which wine tastes good with which food, but when a particular opinion gains acceptance among a sizable enough number of people, that opinion becomes *generally held*, and when a generally held opinion is around long enough, that generally held opinion becomes *right*. And when something is right, everything else becomes *wrong*.

So here we have the key to all of the trepidation that surrounds our dealings with a wine list in a restaurant or a clerk in a wine shop: a leap of illogic by which if a particular pairing of wine and food is thought to be successful and satisfying, then all others are unsuccessful and dissatisfying —to wit, if you are not right, then you are wrong. And who among us needs to have our fallibility put on display, especially at prices upwards of $15 or $20 a bottle?

In fact, even among the arbiters who have formulated the various matches, the choice of which wine goes with which food is nothing more than a personal decision based on a familiarity with the tastes of different wines and the tastes of various foods.

Familiarity with a particular type of food comes from eating it often enough to be able to call up its taste just by thinking of it. Almost all of us do this every day: think of a food that you eat on a fairly regular basis, one of your favorite recipes that you have for lunch or dinner once a week or perhaps two or three times a month. On those days when you know you're going to have it you can pretty much anticipate its taste hours before mealtime, right? Or imagine you're out on your lunch break trying to decide what to eat, and you come to a McDonald's. In your mind you conjure up the taste of a Big Mac and use that to decide if it comes close to what you're in the mood for. If it does, you go in and have lunch; if not, you keep walking and go through the same process at the pizzeria, deli, or hot dog stand farther along the street.

The place into which we reach to pull out the memory of

all those Big Macs, pizzas, and hot dogs is the library of food tastes that we all carry around inside our heads. It's very versatile, and can be used in a variety of ways.

For instance, when you're presented with a dish you've never had before, you use your library of food tastes as a point of reference to form some idea of what the meal will possibly taste like. This is what you do in a restaurant when there is some item or house specialty that you don't know, like Veal Caprice (to make up a name out of thin air for the sake of illustration). You know what veal tastes like, and upon further inquiry you find that it is sauteed and served with mushrooms and pearl onions in a light honey-glaze sauce. You have entries for each of these ingredients stored up in your taste library, and by putting them together in your mind you can decide whether their combination in Veal Caprice will please you.

It is this same process of combining different entries from our taste library that helps us decide what to drink with our food. Putting aside the question of wines for the moment, we never find ourselves at a loss for coming up with some sort of beverage to have with lunch or dinner, be it beer, a soft drink, iced tea, or what have you. Some people will drink the same thing regardless of what is on the plate in front of them, but almost everyone will vary their choice not only to suit the food, but also to satisfy what they feel like having just then. So if one time you opt to have a ginger ale with a pepper steak, the next time you might feel like having a beer. There's no one beverage that is the perfect accompaniment to that steak, is there? So why must there be a perfect wine?

This is not to say that everything will go with anything.

You can drink a variety of things with that steak, but chances are that chocolate milk might not be everyone's first choice. Just as there are certain beverage and food combinations that do not make for the happiest marriages, so there are with wine. In the case of chocolate milk and steak, we know the taste of the food and we know the taste of the beverage, and the mental combination of the two simply doesn't work—for most people, that is.

This is the same process that takes place when deciding which wine to have with which food—the memory of the tastes of different foods are matched up with the memory of the tastes of different wines. Most of us are at a loss here, however, because we have not drunk wine on a regular enough basis to establish any definite impression of what the various types taste like. It is necessary to develop a reference library of wine tastes similar to the ones that already exist for soft drinks, spirits, and other beverages.

Well, the only way to do this is to begin making wine a regular part of your meals. Don't worry about trying to establish a perfect match between what you're eating and what you're drinking at this stage; the important thing is to try and develop some impression in your mind of what a particular type of wine tastes like. Try drinking the same wine with every lunch or dinner for a week or more. If that seems a little monotonous, divide this between two different wines. Drink them until you have a reasonable impression of what those wines taste like, in the same way that you have impressions of what cream soda or scotch tastes like. Then move on and do the same thing with two other wines.

Of course, there will be different winemakers or regions

making wine of any given type, but don't let this throw you. There are also different types of scotch and different makers of cream soda, but your impressions of those beverages are still clear enough to tell when each would be appropriate or satisfying at any given time.

Even as you are creating this library of tastes, you may still find yourself at an occasional loss when making a suitable choice for a food and wine match. Think of this: if you made a list of all the different beverages that would go well with that pepper steak and another list of everything that wouldn't, you'll see that your chances of hitting on a pleasing combination (cola, black cherry soda, beer, sparkling water, iced tea, etc.) are much greater than coming up with something questionable (chocolate milk or orange juice). So understand that the same likelihood exists that you will probably make a good, reasonable choice (remember, there is no "right" choice) in your selection of a wine.

18

Where Do You Go from Here?

You now have a fundamental understanding of wine at least equal to, and perhaps exceeding, that of the average French citizen, Italian, Spaniard, or any of the millions of other people around the world who make a glass or two of wine a daily part of their lives. Although I hope that you will always find some mystery in wine (as in life itself), you should never be afraid or intimidated by it.

At this point, you can do one of two things. You can use this book as a jumping-off point and continue reading whatever you can find about wine. This book is by no means the only wine book you will ever need; there are entire areas of wine and winemaking that have not been discussed here (like grape varieties and their effect on quality and taste) because they were beyond the basic aim of this book. The bibliography will give you some good suggestions for future reading that will build on the knowledge you now have. With each new book and article, your understanding and appreciation for wine will grow, and you may well find yourself devoting more and more time (and money) toward refining your palate and increasing your wine-tasting experience—which, when all is said and done, is the best way to learn about wine.

Or, you can never bother yourself with another book or article about wine and just go right out now and buy a bottle of something to enjoy with your next meal, secure in the knowledge that you're not missing out on some hidden enjoyment that makes wine so special.

Neither choice is necessarily better than the other. Should you decide on the latter, you will certainly enjoy your wine no less than someone who can correctly identify a wine without looking at the bottle—a talent that is little better and not much more useful than a parlor trick, at least until the day they begin shooting people for insufficient erudition in wine.

Should you choose the former, please always remember that there's no virtue in using knowledge about wine to intimidate others. Rather than flaunting your vocabulary or familiarity with vintage chart ratings like the code words of some exclusive fraternity of the vine, try to help others feel at ease with wine and encourage them to appreciate it as you do. As you've seen, there's nothing innately boring or pretentious about wine; there's no reason why anyone should adopt such an attitude about it either.

But most of all, never forget that the important thing about wine is to not forgo the pleasure that it can bring you, a pleasure that is as old as time and as universal as love.

Selected Bibliography

It would be very easy to continue reading about wine for the rest of your drinking days and always learn something new about the subject. Accordingly, I have divided this list into three parts: those books that deal with wine on an introductory level (like this one), intermediate-level books, and advanced titles on the subject. Regardless of their level, all of the books listed below speak simply and intelligently, and will do much to enhance your enjoyment of wine. (Many of the books recommended will have bibliographies of their own that can guide you to other titles you may eventually find useful.)

One or two of the titles that follow are from England and a few others were first published some time ago; consequently, they may be a little difficult to obtain, but it is well worth the effort. Should you have any difficulty in finding these books at your local bookstore or library, there is a excellent specialty shop that can help you obtain these and practically any other books on wine and food:

Kitchen Arts and Letters
1435 Lexington Avenue
New York, NY 10128
(212) 876-5550

One of the criteria for all the books on this list is that they be in English, and there are certainly enough titles published in England and America to keep the most avid reader happily occupied. But I would especially like to mention two excellent books in French that I highly recommend to anyone who reads the language: *Une Initiation à la Dégustation des Grands Vins* by Max Léglise (Marseille: Editions Jeanne Laffitte, 1984); and *Le Vin: Votre Talent de la Dégustation*, by Jean-Claude Buffin (Doussard: Hobby-Vins, 1988). The second book is perhaps the most original and easily accessible (if you read French, that is) introduction to wines that I have ever encountered in any language, and it greatly deserves to be translated into English.

Both of these books are available through Le Verre et L'Assiette, one of Paris' finest gastronomical bookstores.

Le Verre et L'Assiette
1, rue du Val-de-Grâce
75005 Paris
France

Introductory Titles

Clarke, Oz. *The Essential Wine Book*. Rev. ed. New York: Simon & Schuster, Fireside, 1988.
Johnson, Hugh. *How to Enjoy Wine*. New York: Simon & Schuster, Fireside, 1985.
Robinson, Jancis. *Masterglass*. 2d ed. London: Pan, 1987.
Spurrier, Steven, and Michel Dovaz. *The Académie du Vin Wine Course*. 2d ed. New York: Macmillan, 1990.
Zraly, Kevin. *The Windows on the World Complete Wine Course*. Rev. ed. New York: Dell, 1985.

Intermediate Titles

Asher, Gerald. *On Wine.* New York: Random House, 1982.

Johnson, Hugh. *The World Atlas of Wine.* Rev. ed. New York: Simon & Schuster, 1985.

Kramer, Matt. *Making Sense of Wine.* New York: William Morrow & Company, 1989.

Loftus, Simon. *Anatomy of the Wine Trade: Abe's Sardines and Other Stories.* New York: Harper & Row, 1985.

Lynch, Kermit. *Adventures on the Wine Route: A Wine Buyer's Tour of France.* New York: Farrar, Straus & Giroux, 1988.

Wallace, Forrest, and Gilbert Cross. *The Game of Wine.* New York: Harper & Row, 1977.

Advanced Titles

Peynaud, Emile. *The Taste of Wine: The Art and Science of Wine Appreciation.* Translated by Michael Schuster. San Francisco: The Wine Appreciation Guild, 1987.

Robinson, Jancis. *Vines, Grapes, and Wines.* New York: Knopf, 1986.

———. *Vintage Timecharts: The Pedigree and Performance of Fine Wines to the Year 2000.* New York: Weidenfeld & Nicolson, 1989.

Also of Interest

The Wine Spectator. Published biweekly.

Appendix A

Quality Classifications of Various Wine-Producing Countries

Every effort has been made to keep this book as free of foreign terms as possible while still providing the essential information necessary for an understanding of the subject. The terms designating the different qualities of wine produced by each of the major wine-producing nations can easily be translated, but would therefore become practically useless since it is in the original language that they appear on the labels. Their significance is basically uniform and can be easily explained in English, however, so for the sake of convenience they are listed here, in descending order of quality.

France

There are four levels of quality in the French classification system.

Appellation d'Origine Contrôlée (or A.O.C.). Wines qualifying for this classification will have the words "Appellation Contrôlée" on the label. Most of the French wines imported to the United States are in this category.

Vins Délimités de Qualité Supérieure (or V.D.Q.S.). These wines will have a little emblem with the letters V.D.Q.S. displayed on the label. Wines of this quality are relatively rare in the United States.

Vins de Pays (or "Country Wines"). Wines come by this classification in a variety of ways, generally because they come from a region whose quality is not recognized as being the equal of the preceding two classifications. These wines are being imported more and more because of the very good value they represent—while not as good as an A.O.C. wine, the difference in price makes these country wines an excellent value.

Vins de Table (or "Table Wines"). These are common wines that are extremely inexpensive (reflecting the care that goes into their production) and consequently are quite

popular among the indigent class in the streets and sub-
ways of Paris. These wines are virtually never exported
to the United States, and are included in this list only for
the sake of completeness.

Italy

As mentioned in Chapter 11, the French wine laws were the
model for similar legislation in most of the other wine-
producing countries, so the Italian classification system will
closely parallel that listed above.

Denominazione di Origine Controllata Garantita (or DOCG).
This is the highest classification that is only available to
the wines from a very limited number of regions and
signifies that the government certifies the authenticity of
these wines.

Denominazione di Origine Controllata (or DOC). This is similar to the A.O.C. in the French system.

Vino tipici. A "country wine," similar to the French *vins de
pays* designation.

Vino di tavola. "Table wine," similar to the French *vins de
table.*

Spain

Just as we've seen similarities between the French and Italian wine laws, so will we find the same model at work in the
Spanish system of classification.

Denominación de Origen Calificada (or DOCa). This is similar
to the DOCG in the Italian system, and signifies that a

wine so classified comes from a region whose production is of the highest quality.

Denominación de Origen (or DO). Similar to the A.O.C. in France and DOC in Italy. Unique to Spain, however, is the emphasis the authorities place on the length of time a wine has been allowed to age as a determinant of quality:

GRAN RESERVA. For a red wine this signifies that it has spent at least two years in oak casks and three years in the bottle; whites and roses in this category have aged in cask for a minimum of six months and a grand total of at least four years in cask and bottle combined.

RESERVA. Red wines that have spent one year in oak casks followed by at least two years in the bottle; whites and rosés aged a minimum of 24 months, with at least six months in oak casks.

CRIANZA. These wines have followed the aging requirements of the region in which they were produced, which are generally less lengthy than the requirements for Reserva or Gran Reserva wines.

Vino de la Tierra. The Spanish version of "country wine," similar to *vins de pays* or *vino tipici* in France and Italy, respectively.

Vino de Mesa. "Table wine," as in the French *vin de table* and the Italian *vino de tavola.*

Germany

Although there are similarities to the other European classifications, the German system emphasizes the grape's degree of ripeness. In general, the riper the grape, the higher the classification of the wine made from it (and the sweeter it will be).

Qualitätswein mit Prädikat (or simply *"Prädikat"*, meaning "distinction"). This is the classification where the finest German wines are to be found. Prädikat wines are divided into six subcategories:

TROCKENBEERENAUSLESE (or TBA). A very high-quality dessert wine, made from grapes that have attained a great degree of overmaturity.

EISWEIN (or "ice wine"). Another type of high-quality dessert wine, made from grapes harvested after the first frost and pressed while still frozen.

BEERENAUSLESE (or BA). Again, a sweet dessert wine made from very ripe grapes.

AUSLESE. Made from very ripe grapes, usually (but not necessarily) sweet. The term *trocken* on the label signifies that the wine is made in a dry style; *halbtrocken* means half-dry, or only semisweet.

SPATLESE. Wine made from overripe grapes picked after the regular harvest, but not as rich in character as the above categories. These wines can be either sweet or dry.

KABINETT. The grapes for this type of wine are fully ripened and are harvested as soon as they have reached their basic level of maturity. These are the simplest of the Prädikat wines in character.

Qualitätswein bestimmter Anbaugebiete (or QbA). Wine bearing this designation will have the taste and style of wine traditional to the region from which it comes. In other words, "country wine."

Tafelwein (or "table wine"). The most basic category, indicating that the wine was made from normally ripe grapes.

As mentioned on page 65, "estate bottled" is the term used for a wine which has been made from grapes grown and vinified by the same person (or company). The concept is not unique to English-language producers, and other countries have similar terms which are found on the labels of their wines. For instance:

France	*Mis en bouteille au château* or
	Mis en bouteille au domaine
Italy	*Imbottigliato all'origine*
Spain	*Embotellado en la bodega*
Germany	*Erzeugerabfüllung*

Since these terms can be rather distancing for may people, some winemakers and importers will simply substitute or include the words "estate bottled" on wines destined for English-language markets, making it that much easier to be sure of recognizing this level of quality.

Appendix B

Wine Lists— The Bad and the Beautiful

A Typically Bad Wine List

BEAUJOLAIS	$12.50
MONTRACHET, Pierre Morey	150.00
CORNAS, Robert Michel, 1980	25.00
BAROLO RISERVA, 1982/1983	50.00
CHATEAU TALBOT, 1982	60.00
TALBOTT, 1982	60.00
CHATEAU ROTHSCHILD, Pauillac, 1982	175.00

Although there are only seven wines in our abbreviated wine list, it is packed with enough ambiguity, misinformation, and omission to lead to much confusion and possible disappointment.

To begin with, there is no apparent order to the list, thus nothing to tell you where a wine comes from (France? Italy? California?) or even which are the red wines and which are the white.

Second, the Beaujolais and Montrachet do not show a vintage, which is an obvious omission, but the Barolo Riserva shows *two*. Does this mean that when you order this wine you will get to choose which vintage you'd like? (It means that when the wine list was being printed they were about to change from the 1982s to the 1983s, and did not want to bother reprinting the list once the earlier vintage was gone.)

Next, who made the Beaujolais? Depending on the winemaker, the wine may or may not be worth the price they are asking for it and you have no way of knowing until the bottle is brought to the table and you can see the label for yourself.

There is some free-floating ambiguity in the listings for Château Talbot and Talbott. Is the Talbot the same as the Talbott just below it with an extra "t" added to the name by mistake?

And the entry for the Château Rothschild is not entirely accurate: while the list does give the place where the wine comes from (Pauillac), the name of the wine is not complete. Is it *Lafite* Rothschild or *Mouton* Rothschild? Various branches of the Rothschild family own numerous vineyards, each making a distinct style of wine. Simply putting the Rothschild name on the wine list may give it a touch of class, but it shouldn't be forgotten that if the information that the list is to convey is not complete or accurate, it can have all the class in the world but only be suitable for wrapping fish heads in the kitchen.

A Much-Improved Version

Red Bordeaux

CHATEAU LAFITE ROTHSCHILD,
Pauillac, 1982 .... $175.00
CHATEAU TALBOT, St. Julien, 1982 .... 60.00

White Burgundy

MONTRACHET, Pierre Morey, 1983 .... 150.00

Red Burgundy

BEAUJOLAIS, Georges Duboeuf, 1989 .... 12.50

Red Rhone

CORNAS, Robert Michel, 1980 .... 25.00

White Californian

TALBOTT CHARDONNAY, Monterey, 1982 .... 60.00

Red Italian

BAROLO RISERVA, Valentino, 1982 .... 50.00

Here we are able to see at a glance the basic identity of each of the wines on the list, classified by region and color. Each entry has its full complement of information: the wine's name, which town or winemaker made it, and the vintage.

Now there is no confusion about the Château Talbot and the Talbott—it is clear that these are two different wines with no relationship at all. The question about which Rothschild's wine is being offered is answered, and you can be a little more sure which vintage of the Barolo will be coming to the table.

Even with the good wine lists, it still takes a little time and experience to fully understand all that it is telling you, but at least you won't be hindered by misinformation.

Appendix C

Vintage Charts

As mentioned in Chapter 12, vintage charts come in a variety of formats. But regardless of how they are designed and the amount of information they contain, all vintage charts are basically intended to give you an idea of the relative quality of the wine from a given area in a given year. The four charts presented here offer a pretty good sample of the diversity of styles you are likely to encounter.

The Australian chart is a fairly straightforward example which uses numbers as an expression of quality—the higher the number the better the quality of the wine. The left hand column lists the major wine producing regions in that country, and the letters in parentheses are abbreviations for the states in which these regions are located (SA=South Australia; NSW=New South Wales; WA=Western Australia). Notice that there are two ratings for each year, one for red wines and one for white. Since different grape varieties will vary in the degree of ripeness they can attain given the weather conditions during the year's growing season, it is natural to expect that there may be a difference between the quality attained by the grapes used for red wines and those for whites, and therefore in the red and white wines themselves.

The chart for French wines uses a system of dots and stars to express relative quality. This is especially practical in light of the greater number of regions and wine types which are dealt with here. You will see that there are gaps in the sequence of years, and that spaces are left blank in many of the columns—this simply indicates that certain wines are no longer generally available. This points out a basic truth about wine: it is an agricultural product, and when a year's supply runs out it is simply not feasible to go back to the winemaker and say "Could you please grow some more of those grapes the way you did in 1977?" When it comes to wine, when it's gone, it's gone.

The Italian chart, similar in appearance to the French one, offers more than just an assessment of the quality of that country's various red wines from a particular year. Here we are also given a general indication of when each type of wine might best be enjoyed. This can be particularly helpful when trying to decide if you should purchase a particular wine for that evening's dinner. This chart also addresses the exceptions to the rule through the use of circles, triangles, and squares to show departures from the overall aging assessment indicated by the shading in the rating columns.

The German wine chart is the most formidable of the four, not just in its appearance but in the amount of informa-

VINTAGE CHART/AUSTRALIAN WINES

Vintages are assessed out of a possible maximum seven points.
The first mark is for whites, the second is for reds.

YEAR	1970	1971	1972	1973	1974	1975	1976	1977	1978	1979	1980
BAROSSA (SA)	3/7	6/4	5/5	5/7	1/2	3/5	6/7	3/5	5/5	5/6	5/5
CLARE (SA)	4/5	5/6	6/4	5/2	2/3	4/7	4/6	6/5	6/6	4/6	5/5
COONAWARRA (SA)	4/5	5/5	5/6	5/4	5/5	4/6	6/7	4/6	6/6	6/7	6/7
PADTHAWAY (SA)	3/4	5/5	5/5	5/4	5/5	4/5	5/6	4/6	6/6	6/5	6/6
McLAREN VALE (SA)	4/4	5/6	5/5	5/4	4/3	5/6	5/6	4/5	5/5	5/6	5/6
HUNTER (NSW)	4/5	1/2	3/4	4/5	6/4	5/6	6/5	4/4	5/5	6/7	6/6
MUDGEE (NSW)	N/A	1/3	6/5	6/5	6/6	4/5	4/4	5/4	4/6	6/5	5/5
SWAN VALLEY (WA)	2/2	3/2	4/3	5/4	4/4	5/5	3/4	4/5	6/5	5/5	7/5
SOUTHERN (WA)	N/A	N/A	7/3	6/5	5/5	4/6	4/5	5/5	5/6	5/6	4/5
CENTRAL VIC. (Gt. Western, etc)	3/3	5/7	3/2	5/4	4/5	4/5	4/5	5/5	5/5	6/6	5/6
N.E. VICTORIA (Rutherglen etc)	3/4	4/3	4/5	4/5	4/4	6/6	5/5	5/5	5/4	5/5	4/6

Courtesy of the Australian Wine Importers Association, Inc.

VINTAGE CHART/AUSTRALIAN WINES

Vintages are assessed out of a possible maximum seven points.
The first mark is for whites, the second is for reds.

YEAR	1981	1982	1983	1984	1985	1986	1987	1988	1989	1990	1991
BAROSSA (SA)	4/3	6/6	3/3	7/7	7/6	4/5	6/6	5/6	6/6	5/6	6/6
CLARE (SA)	5/6	5/7	3/4	7/7	6/7	4/6	6/6	6/6	4/6	6/6	6/6
COONAWARRA (SA)	6/7	6/6	2/3	5/7	7/7	5/6	6/5	5/5	5/6	6/7	5/6
PADTHAWAY (SA)	6/5	5/6	2/3	5/4	6/5	6/5	6/4	5/6	4/6	5/6	5/7
McLAREN VALE (SA)	4/5	5/6	5/6	6/7	6/5	5/6	6/5	6/6	6/6	4½/6	5/6
HUNTER (NSW)	4/5	6/6	6/6	5/6	6/5	6/5	6/5	5/4	6/5	5/4	6/7
MUDGEE (NSW)	5/5	5/6	5/5	5/6	6/7	4/5	4/5	5/6	6/6	5/6	5½/6
SWAN VALLEY (WA)	6/6	5/6	5/6	6/6	5/6	6/5	6/5	5/4	5/6	6/4	7/6
SOUTHERN (WA)	6/7	6/6	6/7	7/7	7/6	5/6	6/5	5/6	5/5	6/6	7/5
CENTRAL VIC. (Gt. Western, etc)	6/6	6/6	6/7	5/5	6/2	5/5	6/6	6/7	6/6	6/6	6½/6½
N.E. VICTORIA (Rutherglen etc)	4/6	5/5	4/6	5/7	6/5	4/5	5/6	5/6	6/7	6/5	5/7

Courtesy of the Australian Wine Importers Association, Inc.

CHART OF THE COMPARATIVE QUALITIES OF FRENCH WINES

Lesser Year	Average Year	Good Year	Very Good Year	Exceptional Year
•	••	•••	••••	★

Year	Red Bordeaux	Sauternes, Barsac, and other sweet Bordeaux wines	Dry white Bordeaux	Red Burgundy	White Burgundy	Côtes du Rhône crus	Beaujolais crus	Alsace	Pouilly s/Loire Sancerre	Sweet Loire wines	Champagne
1959	•••	••••	•••	★	••					★	
1961	★	★	★	★	•••	★				•••	
1962	•••	•••	•••	•••	••	••••				•••	
1964	•••	••	••	•••	••	•••				••••	
1966	••••	•••	•••	••••	••	••••				•••	
1967	•••	★	••••	•••	••	•••				••	
1969	•	••	••	••••	•••	•••				••••	
1970	★	•••	•••	•••	•••	★				•••	
1971	••••	•••	•••	•••	•••	••••				•••	
1973	••	•••	•••	••	•••					••	
1975	••••	••••	••••	•	••	••				•••	
1976	••••	••••	••••	••••	•••	••••				••••	
1978	••••	•••	•••	★	••••	★				•••	
1979	••••	•••	•••	•••	★	••••				•••	
1980	••	•••	••	••	••	•••				••	
1981	•••	••••	•••	•••	•••	•••		•••		•••	
1982	★	•••	•••	••	•••	•••		•••		••••	
1983	••••	••••	••••	••••	••••	••••		★		••••	
1984	••	••	••	••	••	••		•		••	
1985	••••	•••	•••	★	••••	★	★	★	••••	★	
1986	••••	••••	•••	•••	••••	•••	••	••	••••	••••	
1987	•••	••	•••	•••	•••	•	•	••	•••	•••	
1988	••••	★	•••	★	••••	••••	•••	★	••••	••••	
1989	★	••••	•••	••••	★	•••	•••	★	★	★	
1990	••••	★	•••	••••	••••	•••	••••	••••	★	★	
1991	SMALL PRODUCTION WITH QUALITATIVE VARIATION, ACCORDING TO REGION										

Champagne column note: Vintage Champagne is produced only in the best years, such as 1982, 1983, 1985, 1986. Nonvintage wines are generally blends that reflect the specific house style.

© Copyright Compagnie des Courtiers-Jurés Piqueurs de Vins de Paris

MOST PRESTIGIOUS VINTAGES: 1921, 1928, 1929, 1945, 1947, 1949, 1955.

The value given to each vintage reflects the average for the region.
Remember that it is the exception that proves the rule.

CHART OF THE COMPARATIVE QUALITIES OF FRENCH WINES

Lesser Year	Average Year	Good Year	Very Good Year	Exceptional Year
•	••	•••	••••	★

Year	Dry whites from Loire	Red wines from Loire	Savoie and Jura: Whites and rosés	Savoie and Jura: Red wines	Provence, Côte d'Azur and Corsica: Whites and rosés	Provence, Côte d'Azur and Corsica: Red wines	Languedoc-Roussillon: Whites and rosés	Languedoc-Roussillon: Red wines	South-western France: Whites and rosés	South-western France: Red wines
1959										
1961										
1962										
1964										
1966										
1967										
1969		••••								
1970		•••								
1971		•••								
1973		••								
1975		•••								
1976		••••								
1978		•••								
1979		•••								
1980										
1981						•••			••	•••
1982		•••				••••			••••	•••
1983		•••				•••			••••	••••
1984		••				••			••	••
1985		••••				★		••••	••••	★
1986		••••			••••	•••		•••	•••	••
1987	•••	•••			••	••	••	••	•••	••••
1988	•••	••••	•••	••••	••	•••	•••	••••	••••	•••
1989	••••	★	••••	••••	••	••	•••	•••	••••	••••
1990	••••	••••	★	••••	•••	••••	•••	•••	••••	•••
1991	•••	•••	••••	•••	•	••	•••	•••	••	••

Appellations by column:
- Dry whites from Loire: Anjou, Muscadet, Saumur, Touraine, Vouvray
- Red wines from Loire: Chinon, Bourgueil, Saumur, Champigny, Anjou
- Languedoc-Roussillon: Corbières, Costières de Nîmes, Coteaux du Languedoc, Côtes du Roussillon, Faugères, Fitou, Minervois, Saint-Chinian
- South-western France: Béarn, Bergerac, Buzet, Cahors, Côtes de Duras, Côtes du Frontonnais, Gaillac, Jurançon, Madiran

THE LIST OF APPELLATIONS MENTIONED ABOVE IS NOT EXHAUSTIVE.

The value given to each vintage reflects the average for the region.
Remember that it is the exception that proves the rule.

tion it attempts to convey. Here the wines are classified not only by their region of origin, but also by their grape variety, which as we mentioned above is a prime factor in assessing the quality of a vintage. Furthermore, in addition to informing us how successful the vintage was for a particular grape variety in a given region (indicated by the awarding of one, two, or three solid or open dots), we are also offered an idea of how well the wines were drinking (indicated by the various square and circle symbols) in spring of 1991 when the chart was made. Variation in the development of a region's wines is indicated by the appearance of more than one symbol in some of the columns rating drinkability.

Although at first glance this may all appear somewhat intimidating, remember that the basic principle here is the same as for any vintage chart—to help you determine how satisfying you are likely to find the wines that were made in a particular place in a given year.

Vintage chart of selected Italian red DOC & DOCG wines

WINES / REGIONS	AGLIANICO DEL VULTURE DOC (BASILICATA ◆▲)	BARBARESCO DOCG (PIEDMONT)	BARBERA D'ALBA DOC (PIEDMONT ●■)	BARBERA D'ASTI DOC (PIEDMONT)	BARDOLINO DOC (VENETO ▲)	BAROLO DOCG (PIEDMONT)	BRUNELLO DI MONTALCINO DOCG (TUSCANY)	CANNONAU DOC (SARDINIA)	CARMIGNANO DOCG (TUSCANY ▲)	CASTEL DEL MONTE DOC (APULIA ■)	CHIANTI DOCG (TUSCANY)	CIRÒ DOC (CALABRIA)	COLLI ORIENTALI DEL FRIULI REFOSCO DOC (FRIULI-VENEZIA GIULIA ●)	GATTINARA DOC (PIEDMONT)	GHEMME DOC (PIEDMONT)	GRIGNOLINO D'ASTI DOC (PIEDMONT)	LAMBRUSCO DOC (EMILIA-ROMAGNA ●■)	MONTEPULCIANO D'ABRUZZO DOC (ABRUZZI ●■)	NEBBIOLO D'ALBA DOC (PIEDMONT)	ROSSO CONERO DOC (MARCHES)	ROSSO DI MONTALCINO DOC (TUSCANY ■)	ROSSO PICENO DOC (MARCHES)	SALICE SALENTINO DOC (APULIA ■)	SANGIOVESE DI ROMAGNA DOC (EMILIA-ROMAGNA ●■)	TAURASI DOC (CAMPANIA)	TEROLDEGO ROTALIANO DOC (TRENTINO-ALTO ADIGE ■)	TORGIANO ROSSO RISERVA DOCG (UMBRIA)	TRENTINO MERLOT DOC (TRENTINO-ALTO ADIGE ●■)	VALPOLICELLA DOC (VENETO ●■)	VALTELLINA DOC (LOMBARDY)	VINO NOBILE DI MONTEPULCIANO DOCG (TUSCANY ▲)
1974	1	3	3	4	2	3	1	3	2	4	3	4	4	2	4	4	2	3	–	4	3	–	3	2	4	2	3	3	4	3	1
1975	3	2	2	3	2	4	2	4	4	3	3	2	3	2	2	2	3	–	2	3	–	3	3	2	2	3	4	2	2	3	4
1976	3	2	2	2	2	2	2	2	4	1	2	2	3	3	2	3	2	2	1	–	1	1	2	2	3	1	3	2	1	2
1977	3	2	2	1	2	3	2	2	4	2	3	2	3	1	1	2	3	3	2	3	–	3	3	3	4	2	3	2	3	1	4
1978	3	4	4	4	3	4	3	3	3	3	3	2	3	4	4	3	3	4	3	3	2	3	2	2	2	3	2	2	3	3
1979	2	3	3	3	3	3	3	2	4	3	2	3	2	3	3	3	3	4	2	3	3	3	3	2	3	2	3	3	3	2	3
1980	3	2	2	2	3	2	3	2	3	2	2	3	3	2	3	3	3	2	2	2	2	2	4	3	2	3
1981	3	2	2	2	3	2	3	3	4	3	3	2	2	3	3	3	2	1	3	3	3	3	3	3	2	2	2	3
1982	3	4	4	4	1	4	3	3	3	3	2	2	2	4	4	3	2	4	3	3	2	1	2	3	3	4	2	2	2	2
1983	3	2	2	2	3	3	2	2	4	4	3	2	2	3	3	2	4	3	3	2	2	3	3	3	3	2	3	3
1984	1	2	2	2	2	2	1	4	2	3	1	2	2	3	2	3	2	3	2	3	3	2	1	3	1	3	2	1	2
1985	4	4	4	4	3	4	4	2	4	3	4	2	3	4	2	4	4	3	4	4	3	4	4	3	4	4	3	4
1986	3	3	3	2	3	3	2	4	2	3	3	3	3	3	2	4	3	1	3	3	2	2	3	2	3	2	3	4	3
1987	2	2	2	2	2	3	2	2	2	2	3	3	3	2	2	3	3	2	3	3	4	3	4	1	4	2	2	2	3
1988	3	4	4	4	3	4	4	3	4	3	4	4	4	3	4	4	4	4	4	4	4	4	4	4	4	4	3	4
1989	1	4	4	3	2	4	2	3	1	3	2	3	2	4	4	2	4	1	3	2	–	3	3	3	2	2	3	2
1990	4	4	4	4	4	4	2	4	4	3	3	4	4	3	4	3	4	–	3	4	4	3	4	3	4
1991	3	2	3	2	3	2	3	1	2	4	3	4	4	3	3	–	2	2	3	3	–	4	3	2	3	2	3	4

Key to Vintages: 1 - Fair   2 - Good   3 - Very Good   4 - Exceptional

■ To drink young   ■ Suitable for moderate aging   □ Suitable for long aging

● May also be drunk young   ▲ Sometimes suitable for moderate aging   ■ Sometimes suitable for long aging

Courtesy of the Italian Trade Commission

Vintage Chart for Bottled Wines of Spätlese Quality

from all 13 wine-producing regions in Germany, classified by major grape varieties.
(Spring 1991)

		1983	1984	1985	1986	1987	1988	1989
Rhein-hessen	Müller-Thg.	°°/○ ◗)	○○)	°°/○ ◗	°°/○ ◗	°°/○ ◗	°°/○ ●	°°/○ ●
	Riesling	•• ●◗	°°/○ ◗	•• ◗	•• ●◗	• ●◗	•• ■●	•• ■●
	Silvaner	•• ◗)	°°/○)	••)	• ◗)	• ◗)	• ●	• ●
	Neuzücht.	• ◗)	°°/○)	••)	•• ◗	• ◗)	• ●◗	• ●
Rhein-Pfalz	Müller-Thg.	• ◗)	°°/○)	• ◗)	• ◗	• ◗	•• ●	• ●
	Riesling	•• ●)	• ◗	•• ●◗	•• ●	•• ●◗	•• ■●	•• ▮■
	Silvaner	•• ◗	•)	•• ◗	•• ●◗	• ●◗	•• ●	• ■●
	Neuzücht.	• ◗)	°°/○)	•• ◗)	• ◗	• ◗	•• ●	• ■●
Mosel-Saar-Ruwer	Müller-Thg.	• ◗)	○○ ◗)	•• ●◗	°°/○ ●◗	• ●◗	• ■●	°°/○ ■
	Riesling	•• ◗)	○○ ◗	•• ■●	• ●◗	•• ■●	•• ■●	•• ▮■
Baden	Müller-Thg.	••)	•)	•• ●◗	•• ●◗	°°/○ ●◗	°°/○ ●	• ■
	Ruländer	•• ◗	○○ ◗	•: ●	• ●	• ●	°°/○ ■	•• ■
	Spätburg.	•: ◗	°°/○)	•: ●	°°/○ ●	°°/○ ●	°°/○ ■	•: ■
Würt-temberg	Müller-Thg.	•• ◗)	°°/○ ◗	•• ●	• ●◗	• ▮●	• ●	• ▮
	Riesling	•• ◗)	○○ ◗	•• ●◗	•• ●	•• ▮●	• ■	•• ▮■
	Rote Sort.	•• ◗	○○ ◗)	•• ●	• ▮●	• ▮●	• ■	• ▮
Nahe	Müller-Thg.	•• ◗	°°/○)	•• ■	• ■	• ■	• ●	°°/○ ■
	Riesling	•• ●	°°/○ ◗	•• ●	• ■	• ●◗	•• ●	•• ●

Symbol	Meaning	Symbol	Meaning	Symbol	Meaning	Symbol	Meaning
•:	Very Best Quality	°°	Medium Quality	∣	Needs Aging	●	At Its Peak
••	Very Good Quality	○○	Little Quality	▮	Drinkable Now	◗	Beginning to Decline
•	Good Quality	○	Inferior Quality	■	Mature	)	Past Its Prime

Vintage Chart for Bottled Wines of Spätlese Quality

from all 13 wine producing regions in Germany, classified by major grape varieties.
(Spring 1991)

		1983	1984	1985	1986	1987	1988	1989
Nahe	Silvaner	•• ●	°°/°° ▶	•• ●	• ■	• ●▶	•• ●	• ●
	Neuzücht.	• ●▶	°°/°° ▶)	•• ●▶	• ■	• ■	•• ●▶	• ■●
Franken	Müller-Thg.	•)	°°/°° ▶)	• ▶	• ●▶	°°/°° ●	• ●	°°/°° ●
	Riesling	•• ▶	°° ▶	• ●▶	• ●	°°/°° ●	•• ■	•• ∎
	Silvaner	• ▶)	°°/°° ▶)	• ●▶	• ●	°°/°° ●	•• ●	•• ■
Rhein-gau	Riesling	•• ▶)	°°)	•• ●▶	•• ●	• ●▶	•• ●	•• ■
	Neuzücht.	•)	°°)	••)	• ▶	• ▶	• ●▶	°°/°° ●
Mittel-rhein	Riesling	•• ▶)	°° ▶)	• ●▶	• ●▶	°° ●	•• ■	•• ■
	Neuzücht.	•)	°° ▶)	• ▶	• ▶	°°/°° ▶	•• ●▶	•• ●
Ahr	Müller-Thg.	•)	°°)	• ▶	• ▶	• ●▶	• ●	°°/°° ■
	Riesling	•• ▶)	°° ▶	•• ●▶	•• ● ▶	• ●	• ■●	•• ■
	Spätburg.	•• ▶	°° ▶	•• ●▶	•• ●	• ●	•• ■●	•• ■
Hess. Bergstr.	Müller-Thg.	•)	°°/°°)	•• ▶	°°/°° ▶	• ▶	•• ●▶	• ●
	Riesling	•• ●▶	°° ▶	•• ●▶	• ●▶	• ●▶	•• ■	• ■
Saale/ Unstrut	Müller-Thg.	Wines are no longer available				•	●▶	• ●
	Silvaner					•	●	•• ●
Sachsen	Müller-Thg.	Wines are no longer available				•	●▶	• ●
	w. Burgund.					•	●	•• ■●

•• Very Best Quality	°°/°° Medium Quality	∎ Needs Aging	● At Its Peak
•• Very Good Quality	°° Little Quality	∎ Drinkable Now	▶ Beginning to Decline
• Good Quality	° Inferior Quality	■ Mature	) Past Its Prime

183

Index

A

Acidity
    in red wines, 27, 31
    in white wines, 14–17,
        20–21
Aftertaste, 8–12
Aging, 20, 30–33, 48–49,
        63–64, 130–131,
        139–140
    effect of temperature,
        129–130
    effect of vintage, 113
Alcohol, 19, 58, 74, 77,
        93, 94–95
Appearance
    and quality, 50
Aroma, 49
    effect of breathing,
        138–139
    effect of vintage, 113
    to identify faulty wine,
        148–149

of red wines, 43
of rosé wines, 70
of white wines, 43
Astrodome, 62

B

"Bag-in-a-Box," 86–88
Balance
    in red wines, 29
    in white wines, 15–16,
        18
Barrel aging, 61, 63, 66–
        68
Baseball programs, 142–
        143
Beer, 18, 150
Bottle aging, 63–64, 85,
        87, 128–129, 138
Bread, 48
Breathing, 138–139

A Word About The Type:

The text of *Wine Basics* is set in Ehrhardt, a typeface designed in 1938 under the supervision of Stanley Morison for the Monotype Corporation, based on original fonts used at the Ehrhardt type foundry in Leipzig during the 18th Century. Its subtly condensed design makes it an economical choice for book work, while its generous x-height promotes easy readability. The "Cheers!" sidebars are set in Gill Sans Light, a sans-serif face created, once again for Monotype, in 1927 by Eric Gill. Among the most readable of the sans-serif alphabets produced in the years between the wars, Gill's letterforms balance a measured irregularity in design with the grace of a serif typeface, resulting in a printed page which engages the reader's eye without upstaging the information being conveyed. In addition, the chapter titles and page headings are set in Bulmer Italic, an adaptation of a typeface designed by William Martin around 1790; Fenice Bold Italic, created by Aldo Novarese in 1980, is used for the "Cheers!" headings.